Optimizing
Student Learning

Also available from ASQ Quality Press:

Process Management in Education: How to Design, Measure, Deploy, and Improve Organizational Processes
Robert W. Ewy and Henry A. Gmitro

Continuous Improvement in the Mathematics Classroom
Melody J. Russell

Continuous Improvement in the English Classroom
Janelle R. Coady

Continuous Improvement in the Science Classroom, Second Edition
Jeffrey J. Burgard

Continuous Improvement in the Language Arts Classroom
Vickie Hedrick

Continuous Improvement in the History and Social Studies Classroom
Daniel R. McCaulley

Permission to Forget: And Nine Other Root Causes of America's Frustration with Education
Lee Jenkins

Improving Student Learning: Applying Deming's Quality Principles in the Classroom, Second Edition
Lee Jenkins

Stakeholder-Driven Strategic Planning in Education: A Practical Guide for Developing and Deploying Successful Long-Range Plans
Robert W. Ewy

Charting Your Course: Lessons Learned During the Journey toward Performance Excellence
Robert W. Ewy and John G. Conyers

Running All the Red Lights: A Journey of System-Wide Educational Reform
Terry Holliday and Brenda Clark

ASQ Education School Self-Assessment Guide to Performance Excellence: Aligning Your School and School District with the Malcolm Baldrige Education Criteria for Performance Excellence
Peter G. LaBonte, ASQ

Claire Anne and the Talking Hat
Barbara A. Cleary

Living on the Edge of Chaos: Leading Schools into the Global Age, Second Edition
Karolyn J. Snyder, Michele Acker-Hocevar, and Kristen M. Snyder

Thinking Tools for Kids: An Activity Book for Classroom Learning, Revised Edition
Sally J. Duncan and Barbara A. Cleary

To request a complimentary catalog of ASQ Quality Press publications, call 800-248-1946, or visit our Web site at http://www.asq.org/quality-press.

Optimizing Student Learning

A Lean Systems Approach to Improving K–12 Education

Betty Ziskovsky and Joe Ziskovsky

Introduction by
Norman Bodek

ASQ Quality Press
Milwaukee, Wisconsin

American Society for Quality, Quality Press, Milwaukee 53203
© 2011 by ASQ
All rights reserved. Published 2010
Printed in the United States of America
16 15 14 13 12 11 10   5 4 3 2 1

Library of Congress Cataloging-in-Publication Data

Ziskovsky, Betty.
  Optimizing student learning : a lean systems approach to improving K–12 education /
Betty Ziskovsky and Joe Ziskovsky.
      p. cm.
  Includes bibliographical references and index.
  ISBN 978-0-87389-799-0 (soft cover : alk. paper)
  1. Teaching. 2. Classroom management. 3. Lesson planning. 4. Learning.
I. Ziskovsky, Joe. II. Title.

  LB1025.3.Z57 2011
  371.39—dc22   2010038022

ISBN: 978-0-87389-799-0

Publisher: William A. Tony
Acquisitions Editor: Matt T. Meinholz
Project Editor: Paul O'Mara
Production Administrator: Randall Benson
Cover design: Chris Partyka

ASQ Mission: The American Society for Quality advances individual, organizational,
and community excellence worldwide through learning, quality improvement, and
knowledge exchange.

Attention Bookstores, Wholesalers, Schools, and Corporations: ASQ Quality Press
books, video, audio, and software are available at quantity discounts with bulk
purchases for business, educational, or instructional use. For information, please
contact ASQ Quality Press at 800-248-1946, or write to ASQ Quality Press,
P.O. Box 3005, Milwaukee, WI 53201-3005.

To place orders or to request ASQ membership information, call 800-248-1946. Visit our
Web site at http://www.asq.org/quality-press.

 Printed on acid-free paper

Quality Press
600 N. Plankinton Avenue
Milwaukee, Wisconsin 53203
Call toll free 800-248-1946
Fax 414-272-1734
www.asq.org
http://www.asq.org/quality-press
http://standardsgroup.asq.org
E-mail: authors@asq.org

Table of Contents

Foreword

K–12 education can be viewed as a thirteen-station production line, each station representing a year of foundational learning built upon the cumulative learning obtained from the previous stations. Ideally, students leave the thirteenth station as high school graduates having the benefits of a fully delivered curriculum. However, that is routinely not the case.

Any teacher within the K–12 grade span who completes the delivery of their assigned curriculum is a rarity. This happens for any number of reasons. "Curriculum" is often defined as a textbook. It is easy to see that if a textbook series is utilized across grade levels, it is inherently assumed by textbook authors, as well as the customer school, that each grade level's book will be completed. It just doesn't happen that way. The fact of the matter is that most students advance to next year's curriculum without having finished learning the curriculum they were assigned this year. For core content teachers, this usually means that precious instructional time intended for teaching their grade level's curriculum must be spent in reviewing or actually introducing the previous year's curriculum as necessary foundation learning for this year's content. Cumulatively, over thirteen years, this failure represents significant learning lost.

This story is a fictionalized account of one teacher's effort to complete her assignment and not contribute to this cumulative learning deficiency. Lisa's story is based on actual practice. Her interest in applying process improvement principles to her teaching practice led to an unusual partnership with a continuous improvement specialist. Their collaboration resulted in an innovative application of the lean waste-elimination approach to classroom teaching and learning. It also resulted in Lisa completing the delivery of her entire curriculum within the school year in a way that allowed students to master the material, as evidenced by significant growth in student performance scores on the standardized achievement test in her content area.

The methods and tools described are based on proven lean techniques and sound education practice. There is no reason Lisa's story can not be replicated across America. Wouldn't that be grand?

Acknowledgments

Lean is a commonsense approach to any endeavor. If you get rid of things that aren't necessary to forward the task (waste), you can do the job more efficiently and more effectively. It's an approach that embraces experimentation, actively solicits improvement ideas from everyone, and promotes collaboration and systems thinking.

Learning is a continuous improvement process. It's all about embellishing and refining existing understanding. So introducing lean into a K–12 classroom was not the result of a clairvoyant Eureka! moment—it was, in assessing the task ahead, simply the most logical way to accomplish the goal of learning. As much as I as the teacher put into the lean implementation, my students put in more. What they did with their empowerment as lean practitioners was what optimized our success. Stepping up to the plate as equal partners in teaching and learning, it was the students who provided the critical feedback on what was working and what wasn't, offered the creative ideas for how to forward learning, and embraced their newfound power to improve themselves. To all of my students over the years who enlightened me on how learning progress is made and life skills are built using lean, this book is dedicated, with both gratitude and my enduring affection.

—Mrs. Z

We would like to acknowledge those who contributed their assistance and support to the success of our endeavor.

To our children, Mary, Joe, Betsy, and Michael—we thank you all for your continued encouragement and feedback both in the concept development and throughout the writing process.

To the educator visionaries who enthusiastically advocate for the powerful potential they see in lean as an approach to better the education process—we so appreciate your support, recommendations, suggestions, and thought-provoking questions. Outstanding for the many phone and written conversations and detailed feedback are Boyce Heidenreich, whose dual insight as both teacher and administrator was invaluable, as well as Melissa Unklesby, a constant source of inspiration and encouragement. Special thanks to Norman Bodek, whose enthusiastic support provided energy to the project and whose personal involvement and newfound friendship we value more than words can say.

We also would like to acknowledge the contributions of the professional educators who reviewed the book and offered constructive feedback, thought-provoking rhetorical questions, and a mix of healthy challenge as well as unwavering belief in the value of the application of lean to K–12 education: Dr. Mary Jane Guy, Professor of Education Leadership, Winona State University; Dr. Peter Ward, Richard Ross Chair in Management, Fisher College of Management, Ohio State University, and Chairman of the LEAN Academic Network; Ken W. Getkin, Chairman American Society for Quality STAR Team, Advisor and Judge for Education Quality Team of Excellence Award. Thanks also to a special group of educators within this category who provided verification feedback on their own classroom lean implementation: Ed Steinmetz, middle school teacher; Melissa Unklesby, middle school teacher; Todd Trick, elementary school teacher; Amy Barlow, secondary school teacher; Richard Pierce, secondary school teacher; Tim Shuman, secondary school teacher; Kim Morton, secondary school teacher; Teri Fisch, middle school teacher; Kerry Davis, teacher. Also thanks to Kathy Rowe for her service as devil's advocate, and to Paul Johnson and Corky Cavanaugh who offered their feedback as lean trainers.

Lastly, our sincere appreciation to Matt Meinholz of ASQ Quality Press, whose belief in the book and passion to get its message out offered a partnership we could not pass up.

—Betty and Joe Ziskovsky

Introduction

I started Productivity Press, Inc. in 1979, went to Japan and discovered the Toyota Production System (JIT or lean), and published close to 250 books on the best of Japanese management practices. Most recently, I taught a course on Japanese management at Portland State University. After my first trip to Japan (75 to date) I became fascinated with finding ways to help American organizations improve their efficiency and effectiveness in producing their products and services. At first we thought that lean only applied to manufacturing companies, but through the years we found that the concepts can be understood and applied in any industry, including many hospitals. And now along comes this wonderful book on how to begin to apply lean to teaching and educating students.

This is really where lean should have started.

If you ask a manager what is their most important asset, they would invariably say, "people." But, ironically, people are not found on a financial balance sheet. You can find inventory, machines, products, investments, but not people. Nor are the majority of workers treated as valuable participants in the process of producing products or delivering services. I think it all starts with our educational system.

So, happily, we finally have an easy-to-read but very interesting book written by Betty and Joe Ziskovsky on how to apply lean principles to the field of education. The heart of lean is the elimination of "muda"—wastes— and the biggest waste is the underutilization of people's talents. This is what the authors address, and to educate students properly, first the teacher has to be proficient in the planning and organizing of the course material.

We learn from the authors: how to improve our skills, to manage time, load leveling, planning the year ahead to insure that instruction is balanced and everything is covered in a way that ensures students master the material. As a teacher, I learned from the book the power of giving weekly tests to see that real learning was taking place "exactly when it is needed, in the right quantity, and at the highest level of quality."

We can see how 5S works in the classroom, how standardized work applies, how to measure the progress of learning, and how to use plan–do–check–adjust (PDCA) to improve both the teaching and learning processes.

So, read the book slowly; have fun and see lean brighten the days for all of your students.

Norman Bodek
President, PCS Inc.
Former owner of Productivity Press, Inc.
Author of *How to Do Kaizen*

What Is Lean?

*L*ean is a term used to describe a value-added approach to process management of personal and work tasks. It considers the expenditure of time, effort, money, or other resources for any goal other than the creation of value as it is perceived by the customer/end user to be wasteful, and thus a target for elimination.

HOW CAN LEAN BE APPLIED TO EDUCATION?

Lean is a program of organizational improvement that empowers each and every worker in a school system—from student through superintendent—to increase his or her personal performance and job satisfaction through process improvement. Lean engages everyone in streamlining his or her work processes by identifying and eliminating the steps within each process that are wasteful, unnecessary, or do not contribute value to—and may even prohibit the person from doing or completing—the work. By incorporating a value-adding approach systemwide, schools can become more efficient in their operations and more effective at delivering their services, optimize the learning performance of all students, and create a culture of success and satisfaction for all.

HOW IT ALL BEGAN

The school year was coming to an end for Metro Middle School. Students had been dismissed for the summer the previous afternoon. This morning, Todd, the principal, gathered his faculty in the library for a final staff meeting before they tackled the breakdown and cleanup of their classrooms. Routine end-of-the-year housekeeping items had been addressed, and the final topic of discussion on the agenda was a familiar one at this time of year, namely, whether students at each grade level had learned everything they were supposed to.

"Well, we had to spend a tremendous amount of time on research writing. I tried to get everything in, but there just wasn't enough time to get everything done," commented Margaret, an eighth-grade Language Arts teacher.

"We covered probably three-fourths of the science text," added Judy.

"I didn't even get to start the sixth-grade math curriculum in my low class until December so, no, they don't have what they should have," stated Don.

Todd looked around the room of tired faces. "Why do you think this is happening? And what are we going to do to correct it?"

The group was silent for a few moments.

"These kids come in with learning deficits that we have to take time to shore up. If they had learned what they were supposed to in the previous grades we wouldn't be having this discussion," piped in Leo, the PE/English instructor.

"All these pullouts are stealing instructional time. I can't get everything done!"

The floodgate was opened, and Todd heard all too clearly how things outside of classroom control were preventing the full scope of learning from happening. However, Lisa, a seventh-grade Social Studies teacher, offered a different insight.

"I couldn't complete my curriculum either. As other people have pointed out, there really were a lot of interruptions to our instructional time. That needs to be addressed. But I think I have to shoulder some responsibility for what happened or didn't happen in my classes. Personally, I'm pretty exasperated with myself. I know there are things beyond my control, but I'm not sure I managed the things within my control very well. After we hit mid-April, and I saw where I wasn't in the curriculum schedule, I started questioning whether I had planned and managed my time well enough. Frankly, I'm frustrated and disappointed in myself for being in this boat two years in a row now."

"You can't plan around everything, Lisa!" admonished Colleen, her Social Studies colleague. "We all just have to do the best we can."

"But that's just it, Colleen," interrupted Lisa. "I'm not so sure that what I've been doing is the best that I can do."

"What do you mean?" Todd interjected.

"Well, as part of my master's coursework I have been reading about this *lean* approach used in manufacturing and now in service industries like healthcare, insurance, and law enforcement. In fact, I've been thinking about this a lot lately, and I've come to the conclusion that education really is a combination of developing and constructing a product and processing a lot of paperwork."

"What!?" Several voices exploded simultaneously.

Lisa patiently went on. "Think about it for a moment. What we do is take a student at a given stage of education and add prescribed learning—our individual curriculum—that ultimately results in the development and production of an educated individual. We're all part of a thirteen-year production line, and each of us is responsible for doing the work assigned to one of those thirteen years."

"You can't be serious!"

"I sure am!"

"So what does this have to do with our problem?" asked Judy.

"It has everything to do with it," explained Lisa. "We did not deliver our product—a student educated to grade-level standards—on time in a complete form. It's just like ordering a car and not getting it when promised, and when you got it, it was missing items you ordered."

"Lisa, I think you've flipped. We all tried, but none of us, including you, got the curriculum done," countered Judy.

Intrigued, Todd interjected, "Lisa, what do you propose we do?"

"From my reading, and in discussing how lean works with actual practitioners, I think a tool that is used to smooth production might be useful to us in helping us keep on track so we can complete our curriculum by year's end. It will mean some changes in how we plan and deliver our instruction, and even how we interact with the students, but I think it will work."

"Learning doesn't work like a production line!" insisted Leo.

Disgruntled mumbles rose from within the group. "This will just mean more work for us, and just like every other new idea, it won't work anyway."

Todd quieted the group. He wanted to hear more, and encouraged Lisa to explain further.

"It is called *level loading*. I propose we take one class and apply this tool and its techniques as a trial for next year."

"Oh yeah, who has the time to do that?" blurted Leo.

Skepticism abounded.

"It won't work!"

"Nobody has ever done it, so how do you know it will even work?"

"I am uncomfortable changing what I have done all these years without proof."

Committed to exploring improvement possibilities, Todd took a positive and supportive stance. "Lisa, since this is your idea, are you willing to develop and pilot this in one of your own classes starting in the fall?"

Lisa nodded her acceptance of the challenge.

"Well, then, we are done here, folks," concluded Todd. "Thank you all for the hard work and dedication you've put in throughout the year. I appreciate your efforts very much. Don't forget to turn in your grade books and student files before you leave, and have a great summer!" Then turning to Lisa, he added, "Can you come down to my office for a few minutes? I'd like to hear more about your idea."

Seated in her principal's office and encouraged by his interest, Lisa briefly explained that the load leveling tool she wanted to apply was a technique used to smooth out the flow of work to help keep a process on schedule. "That's essentially the problem everyone, including me, was talking about, Todd. Interruptions in the teaching schedule have prevented the curriculum delivery process from being completed," she pointed out.

"I'm looking at what I can do to reduce those interruptions for next year, but I simply can't eliminate all of them," replied Todd.

"I know," Lisa assured him, "but I think load leveling will help me plan more effectively for them and how to work around them. And if this will enable us to complete each year's curriculum, then everyone will be able to start the year teaching their assigned curriculum rather than finishing up the curriculum from a previous year."

"Yes, I can definitely see the longitudinal benefit if it works. Okay, Lisa, let's try it. I'll give you the summer to develop your plan. I know your stated goal is to finish delivering your assigned curriculum, but it has to be done in such a way that the kids learn it."

"Oh, yes, the student mastery component is equally important to me in this."

"What class do you propose to pilot this in?"

"Well," Lisa thought out loud, "I think I'd like to tackle World Geography. No one who has taught that class here has ever completed the curriculum, including me. I'd like to see if I can be the first. Plus, as you know, our school score in Geography on the state performance assessment was in the 'Needs Improvement' category. If I can finish the curriculum, I'm sure our score will be higher. We can easily measure whether I complete the curriculum, and next year's school score in Geography will tell us whether or not learning was improved at the same time."

"That sounds like a good check," agreed Todd. "Is there anything further I can provide or do to support you in this? I want you to be able to succeed."

"I know you do. I'd like to be able to get into the building during the summer to have access to everything while I work on this."

"That's fine, keep your key. You just won't have access on weekends."

"Thank you, Todd. I can't think of anything else right now," replied Lisa, "but I'll let you know if I do. I just need to figure out how to do this. I have a friend who is a lean master, and he has been explaining to me how this load leveling works in his business. He has volunteered to be my lean teacher and coach to guide me if I want to try it. I know already it is going to be a lot of work. He has said that most of the effort is in the pre-planning. We both know this will have to be a collaborative learning effort—he will be learning about the education process, and I will learn how to improve my abilities and complete the curriculum on time, completely, and with student mastery. That is my goal."

"And it's an admirable one! We do have some finite funds for professional development of this nature. I will e-mail you with the amount of subsidy I can offer. Keep me updated on your progress, Lisa, and let me know if you need anything during the summer. I'm proud of you for taking this on—it shows real educational leadership." Todd walked Lisa to the door. "Good luck."

Lisa smiled. "Thank you. I have every confidence that this is going to work, Todd."

EMBARKING ON THE JOURNEY

Two weeks later, Lisa welcomed Bill, her lean mentor and coach, to her classroom for their first work session. Bill began by refreshing his friend's understanding of what level loading is and how it could be used in delivering a course of study.

"*Level loading,* or *balanced production* as it is sometimes called, is a method used to balance the production process or, in this case, to balance your curriculum delivery so that you can complete it within the defined school year. Do you remember our talks about the importance of understanding process?"

Lisa nodded, recalling their previous discussions.

Bill quickly reviewed the concept. "Everything we do is a process. Making a sandwich is a process. Filling up your car with gas is a process. Grading papers is a process. Understanding the concept of *process* is critical to any lean improvement activity. You have to understand what a process is before you can see one, and you must be able to visualize a process as a series of steps from beginning to end before you can adjust any of those steps to make an improvement. Do you feel comfortable from our previous conversations that you understand that concept of process?"

"Yes."

"Great. Then what you need to do first is define the specific process that will be the target of your improvement project. And that process would be . . . ?" Bill's voice trailed off as he awaited her answer.

Lisa looked quizzical. *Process . . . ?* She thought. "I teach, they learn, Bill. I have to teach the scope and sequence of material, the curriculum for the grade and course."

"Have you identified the course that we are going to work on?" asked Bill.

"Yes, Social Studies. World Geography is the class I'm targeting."

"Tell me what you have to teach for this course."

"There are a lot of things—people, maps, culture, history—a lot of things. What does what I actually teach have to do with lean or load leveling?"

"You'll be surprised. What you have to teach has everything to do with lean and load leveling, as you will see. Is there a curriculum right now for this class?"

"Yes, sort of." Lisa retrieved a large textbook from a bookshelf across the room and handed it to Bill. "This is the text, and there are additional support materials that we can also use, but we never get through it all."

"Why?"

"Because there is so much to cover, I guess. Then there are interruptions during the year, tests to give, grades to prepare, and . . . well, I guess I really don't know the real reason. We just don't."

Bill explained that load leveling starts by defining what needs to be accomplished, what tasks have to be done, and within what time period. "Then you have to look at what has prevented you from accomplishing this before. What got in the way? What interruptions happened? Why could you not complete the book? Afterwards," Bill continued, "you have to set your goal—where you want to be. That goal we're going to call the 'ideal state' because that's where, ideally, you want to be at the end of next year, right?"

Lisa had already identified her ideal state. "I definitely know my ideal state, Bill. My goal is to complete the World Geography curriculum by the end of the school year with the students achieving mastery learning."

"All right, completing the delivery of your curriculum by the end of the year with all your students understanding the material will be your ideal state. So now we have to figure out all of the processes and activities that are necessary to achieve that goal."

"This is sounding bigger than I thought it might be," said Lisa apprehensively. "All of the processes and activities? I don't even know where to start!"

Bill chuckled. "Hey, do you trust me to guide you through this?"

"Well, yes, but . . . ."

"No buts, Lisa. I'm here to help you, and I assure you that this will not be as hard as you think. Like I told you before, it will require some work, especially the up-front and planning work. We'll just take it step by step."

Lisa was determined to proceed and succeed. "Okay, Bill, where do we begin?"

"First step—define what work needs to be done. Talk to me about what you truly have to accomplish in teaching this course and having the kids learn that material."

Lisa took the textbook from Bill. "This is the book that we are currently using. At a minimum I need to cover the entire book." She flipped through pages, stopping at intervals to show Bill examples of what she was referring to at various stages of her explanation. "For each geographical area I have students do topographical maps like these. There are over 200 countries represented in this book. We need to discuss the customs of various peoples, government types, economics, the political atmosphere, current events, history, and natural resources of the areas. I'm also required to assess understanding at sufficient intervals to determine a grade for the report card. I have to work around interruptions, not all of which I will be able to anticipate. And because my class won't be the only one the students take, I have to be mindful of the amount of homework I ask them to do."

Bill nodded in understanding. "Then let's proceed by going through the book and breaking it up into manageable pieces. How many weeks do you have to work with?"

"I don't know; let me get the school calendar." Lisa rifled through a stack of papers on her desk. Not finding what she was looking for, she picked up a second stack lying next to her computer and searched through them. "I can't seem to find it. I know they were handed out at the last staff meeting and I thought I put everything from the last day on my desk. It has to be here somewhere."

"I see an initial opportunity to help us in the future," chuckled Bill.

"Yes? What's that?" Lisa asked absentmindedly as she searched through the first stack of papers a second time.

"Organization. In the lean world we call it *5S.*"

Her brow wrinkled in confusion as she glanced quickly over at Bill. "5S? Is that some sort of code word?"

Bill chuckled once again. "Nope. It stands for *sort, set in order, shine, standardize,* and *sustain.* It's a workplace organization methodology that will help you find things faster, keep them organized, and reduce the frustration you are experiencing right now. It can be used anywhere, and has been—even in a classroom like this. I'll tell you what, Lisa, let's spend the rest of our time today identifying and going through all the things you feel you need to teach this class and get them organized for ease of use and reference."

With Bill's guidance, Lisa examined every book, note, reference material, and artifact that she had collected to teach her World Geography class and explained to him how she used each resource. They organized everything in a logical manner, with those items needed most frequently located closest to Lisa's desk and those not needed as often stored and labeled for quick recall. In doing this activity, they discovered the missing school calendar, which Lisa posted on the wall closest to her desk where she could view it easily. Bill explained the need for quick access to the calendar, as it would be a core asset in developing the new curriculum sequence.

"There," Bill admired as he stepped back to view the results of several hours of their effort, "doesn't that look better? Everything is organized and ready for use." Lisa had to agree. "Let's call it a day. Tomorrow we'll begin to dig deeper into what can be done. I'll be over after lunch."

"Thanks, Bill. See you tomorrow." Lisa plopped on the edge of her work table and surveyed the progress they had made so far. She sighed. *What have I gotten myself into?* she wondered.

The next morning, Lisa decided to get a jump on things. She dug out her new planner for the coming year, retrieved the calendar from the wall where she had mounted it the day before, and began transferring key school dates into the planner as she had always done. She noted the abundance of scheduled interruptions for this upcoming year—class pictures, holidays, conferences, teacher retreat days, testing days, and so on. *Well this ought to show me what I have left to work with,* she thought. Not knowing what Bill was going to ask her to do next, but remembering his statement that by being organized she would save time, Lisa continued to reorganize her teaching and classroom materials by geographical area.

DEFINING THE CURRICULUM

Time passed quickly for Lisa. Before she knew it, the morning had come and gone. Bill arrived with a "How's it goin'?" He surveyed the newly stacked and labeled bins on the shelves underneath the windows in Lisa's classroom and nodded his approval. "Looks like you've been working already. I'm impressed!"

Lisa stood up and wiped a wisp of hair from her forehead as she beamed. "Yup, I'm already ahead of you in getting organized." She pointed to the stacked bins. "All my artifacts are sorted by geographic area there, and over here"—she pulled out several file drawers in sequence—"I have all the maps, tests, and readings, also sorted and labeled and in one location."

"Well, you have been a busy lady. This will make it much easier for you to access what you need quickly. That's what lean is all about, Lisa—eliminating wastes of time and effort so you can do your job better and easier."

"Bill, I haven't even had to use these things yet and I already know it will be easier for me. Yesterday, this stuff was all over my room and in other locations, too. Now, it's all logically arranged and labeled. I can find any-thing in less than a minute."

"It's going to be easier for your students, too," added Bill. "Just wait and see. Well, this is good that you are ahead of the game because today we have a lot of decisions to make."

"Decisions?"

"Yup! Some will be easy, but others will need some thought, and I guarantee that you will change your mind at least once as we go along."

"Okay, where do we start?"

"With the curriculum."

"The curriculum?"

"Didn't you tell me the book was the curriculum?"

"Yes, it's a major part of it."

"So let's start by going though the book and see what we have to deal with."

Lisa pulled the textbook from her bookshelf and handed it to Bill. "Do you normally just start going from the front to the back," he asked her, "or do you jump around?"

Lisa explained that she normally started the course by covering the North American continent and that her students' interest and background influenced what she covered next. "It doesn't make any difference to me in what order I teach these countries. I try to engage student interest by covering countries from their family backgrounds next. I normally plan my syllabus for the next week on Sunday."

"Did that work?" asked Bill.

"In the short term, but it obviously didn't work for the whole year since I never completed the book."

"How do you think you could have done that better?"

Bill's question caught Lisa by surprise. She thought a moment. "Better? I'm not sure."

"Let me ask the question in a different way. What do you think you could do so that you can get through the entire curriculum given the time constraint you have? Remember, we can't change the calendar."

"How well I know that! And that is where I am ahead, Bill. I have laid out the school calendar in my planner already." She proudly handed him her planner, updated with the prescheduled school events from the next year's calendar. "To answer your question, I suppose I could predetermine the direction for the year and plan farther ahead. But when things change in the schedule I end up replanning and replanning."

"Can you plan for changes?"

"Maybe. It depends on the change, I guess."

"Keep that thought in the back of your mind, Lisa," Bill advised, "but let's go back to my original question and expand on your answer. Taking into account that there will be some lost time due to unforeseen changes and that there may be some short weeks, what keeps you from planning the whole year? What would that look like if you tried it right now?"

Lisa was puzzled. She had not thought about planning out the entire year. *How could you do that not knowing unanticipated schedule changes and the pace of student learning? It would be impossible or at least difficult to do.* "I guess I would first have to look at all the countries and areas that I have to teach. Some have more detail to cover; some could be combined with others that are similar."

"That is our start," commented Bill. "But before we do that, we need to think about the interval over which you will teach a set of countries or areas."

Lisa reached into the small refrigerator she kept on top of her filing cabinet and pulled out a can of root beer and offered it to Bill, who accepted it with thanks and popped the top. Lisa retrieved a can for herself, opened it, and took a drink. "Interval? What do you mean by interval, Bill? I have to teach it all if I am going to complete the curriculum."

Bill sipped his soda, then nodded. "I know you do. I'm asking how long do you need to teach a country, do maps, and discuss politics and all the other things you listed yesterday. Do you need a day, two days, a week, two weeks—how long? What period of time do you feel would be best for you to teach the curriculum completely and for your students to learn it?"

The clock ticking was the only sound in the classroom as Lisa contemplated Bill's question. "Best for me and my students? Probably for me, a week or two; for the students, I don't know. I never thought about it from that perspective."

Bill explained that in manufacturing, lean looks at satisfying the customer and eliminating things that prevent them from being satisfied. "The students are your customers. They need to learn. What is the best way for them to learn and be successful? I think you called it *achieving mastery*. From the student's perspective, what do you think would be the best period of time for them to learn a given amount of material? How would you structure that period of time to give them the best chance for achieving mastery?"

Lisa took another drink of her root beer and looked out the window as she pondered the problem Bill posed. She recalled an insight gained from her graduate studies. "Actually, the needed time should be a function of the amount of material and impression potential."

"Huh?"

A smile spread across Lisa's face as a learning connection to the past shed light on the present problem. "The answer," she explained, "is based in learning theory."

BILL'S FIRST LESSON

It was Bill's turn to knit his eyebrows and look perplexed. "Learning theory? What is that?"

Lisa straightened herself. "Now I get a chance to teach you something!"

"Absolutely! I definitely need to understand more about this. It may be key to creating an effective load leveling plan. I'm all ears, Lisa."

"Learning theory is the general consensus of how people learn based on interpretation of research. This may surprise you, Bill, but teachers don't teach people. People teach themselves by making connections between what they already know and what they don't know. The role of a teacher, then, is to be a catalyst for learning rather than someone who gives knowledge to another. Teachers create the opportunities for students to make learning connections. To effectively create those opportunities, educators must understand and employ *learning theory,* which consists of three elements: 1) brain theory, 2) learning style theory, and 3) the creation of a supportive, trusting relationship between the student and the teacher, which leads to a higher level of learning."

"*Respect for people* and *developing trust* are core tenets of lean, Lisa," concurred Bill. "You mentioned brain theory—is this a theory or a proven concept?"

"Brain theory relates to how brains in general absorb information and is based on actual research findings. Brain theory states that brains absorb more information through small, constant feedings of information rather than one large inundation of it. When a ton of information is presented at one time, the brain can not retain all of it. A good analogy is what happens when a dry sponge is placed under a running faucet of water. When the rush of water hits the sponge, some is absorbed up to the point of saturation while the vast majority of it will just roll off and go down the drain. The point here is that information inundation—cramming—is a waste of time and effort. Brains aren't designed to work like that."

"I'll vouch for that," Bill replied. "I remember I did a lot of cramming in college, but I don't remember much of that book learning."

"And that's exactly the point of brain theory and the findings of brain research, Bill. Related research in advertising reveals what it takes to retain information in long- and short-term memory and be able to accurately recall that information. Getting things stored in long-term memory is facilitated by a series of impressions of the information. An impression is a single feeding of the information. It can be visual, as when we see or read something. It can be an auditory impression, such as when we hear the information. Many people find that physically doing something with or handling the information to be learned in some way makes a very lasting impression."

"I know I remember things best when I write—I take notes on everything," Bill mused.

"And writing notes is a combination of two or more of those senses—you're either listening to or viewing the information and then you touch the pen or pencil and kinesthetically move it to write. Writing is proven to have a superior value in making an impression to just seeing or hearing since it involves two level thinking: the receiving and analysis of the information for what is important enough to write down, and the action of forming the words and thoughts you write as notes. The important thing is that four impressions of the information must be made to get it into short-term memory."

"But what about mastery learning? Doesn't that mean you need to have the information in your long-term memory?" interrupted Bill.

"Actually, yes," continued Lisa, "and you're a step ahead of me. Research shows that a minimum of ten impressions of the same information are necessary for information to be stored in long-term memory."

Bill looked surprised. "Ten impressions?! I'd be bored hearing or seeing or writing or even doing the same thing ten times."

"Of course you would, and it would be pretty difficult to keep paying attention through all ten, too! Research also shows that your brain requires novelty to keep paying attention. So that means if you are going to get ten impressions of the same thing, the only way to keep your brain paying attention to get those ten impressions is to vary the type of feed and the format. So you might read or view something, then the next impression might be writing notes like you do, then a third could be reading those notes out loud to yourself, or having someone read to you so you could listen.

Another impression could be manipulating flashcards with the information so there's a kinesthetic action involved. The goal is to think about the information in different ways and in different formats a total of ten times. But each impression must be totally separated from the others in time."

"I'm not sure I understand the time thing."

Lisa picked up the textbook on her desk and randomly opened the book to a page that was entitled "Angola" and held it up for Bill to see. "If you sat here and read this section on Angola in the textbook, and then I immediately read it to you, and while I was reading you took notes, and then you read those notes back to me, and those things happened one after the other, Bill, your brain would deal with them as one single impression delivered simultaneously in four different formats."

"The combination of senses you mentioned."

"Precisely. If you had separated each of those formats by a couple of hours, they would have counted as different impressions. Impressions also must be separated by sleep periods."

"What?" Now Bill was confused.

"Your brain processes new information during the next sleep cycle. That's why it's virtually impossible to get something into long-term memory in a day. You literally do have to sleep on information to really learn it."

"Lisa, I'm getting a whole new appreciation for what goes into teaching and learning. It isn't as simple as I thought."

Bill's new teacher smiled. "Oh, there's even more. Another finding of brain research is that people learn best when there is a pattern, especially a repeating pattern. And remember, brain theory is only one of the components of learning theory."

"What's the difference between brain theory and learning theory, then?"

"Learning theory states that each individual has a unique set of intelligences or talent areas for processing information to understanding. Every individual learns in a way that is unique to their personality. The way a person learns is commonly referred to as his or her *learning style*. To truly provide value-added educational service to all students, a teacher has to present information in a way that gives the opportunity for all students to learn in his or her best way. Good teaching should include diverse offerings of those ten impressions to ensure that all students' learning styles are used. That way each student has the best chance of reaching the goal of learning mastery. That is learning theory at the high level. How it is actually facilitated and the time required for that facilitation—which is what you are asking me—depends on the teacher and the students. Brain theory says we need to provide a constant, steady flow of information that can easily be absorbed by the brain. Learning theory says we need to embed ten impressions of what is to be learned in that flow using the various intelligences to support and empower the students to learn. And the trust relationship makes it all possible. So the answer to your question of how much time I need to teach for the kids to master the material," concluded Lisa, "is the amount of time in which I can successfully facilitate ten impressions of it."

ESTABLISHING THE SYLLABUS

"So what I heard you say, Lisa, is that not only do we have to consider the amount of material to be covered in this book, there's also the need to build in time for those ten impressions to be made. Is that right?" Bill asked.

Lisa nodded. "You've got it."

"What you just shared with me about impression time is going to be core to creating your load leveling plan. And I want to tell you right now that I still think it can be done successfully to meet your goals. It sounds like you *do* see the student's perspective as well as your own, which is essential. So let's go back to my initial question. What is the best interval for you to teach and the students to learn?"

Lisa pondered that question for a few more moments, then vocalized her thinking so Bill could follow her rationale. "The longer the teaching interval, the more information is shared, and the more information that is shared, the more impressions that interval must include. I'm thinking the interval has to be a week, for manageability for both me and the students, Bill. If I design my curriculum delivery in weekly increments, I think it would be possible within that week to arrange for ten impressions without the kids being overwhelmed. If I can do that, it should work, at least theoretically. But then the next concern I have is whether there are enough weeks to do it that way."

Bill followed Lisa's analysis of the problem and applauded her. "Lisa, welcome to the world of systems thinking!"

Lisa's brows knit in apparent confusion. "Systems thinking?"

"That's right. You are now seeing this problem from the long-term perspective of the entire school year rather than the short-term perspective of one week as you had previously done. And because of that paradigm shift in your thinking, you are now viewing the problem in a more holistic way," Bill explained. "Before, your continuum of thinking about curriculum was from one Sunday to the next. You already admitted that limited vision didn't result in a very successful overall outcome. Now you are thinking about curriculum delivery in terms of the whole school year. I assure you, the broad approach will always significantly increase your chances of success. By the way, your logic in selecting the week as your interval makes perfect sense. Interval is a critical component of load leveling. In my world, interval is referred to as *takt time*."

Before Lisa could put words to the confusion on her face, Bill went on. "*Takt time* is a lean term for a repetitive, set time frame in which the same or similar work will be done."

"But I'm going to be doing a different set of countries every week, Bill."

"Yes, you will, Lisa, but what you do in your teaching may be the same. Didn't you tell me before that you incorporate brain theory in your teaching?"

"Yes, but . . . ."

"And didn't you tell me that part of brain theory is that people learn in patterns?"

"Yes."

"Then I suspect that even if you teach about a different set of countries from one week to the next, the pattern of how you teach and the materials and activities you use will essentially be the same. Is that a correct assumption on my part?"

I guess that's true, Lisa admitted to herself as she recalled how she structured her units. *There really is a pattern to what I do regardless of the particular area of focus or the materials.* She used lectures, artifacts, audiovisuals, maps, and readings as teaching materials. She also had her students review current events, research and discuss a dilemma, and create a topographical map as weekly assignments. "You know, that is a correct assumption, Bill. I never realized it before. But there is a pattern to how I structure and deliver elements of the curriculum."

"Well, your brain research as well as business research support the same conclusion, and that is that using patterns optimizes learning as well as work. Grab your planner, Lisa, and let's take a look at it."

Bill and Lisa moved two chairs in a side-by-side orientation at the large classroom work table.

"So you have already entered the scheduled activities on the school calendar into the planner, right?"

Lisa nodded.

"Let's review it and see how many total weeks you have to work with."

Lisa flipped through the planner pages, counting the weeks as she turned each page. "There are 41 weeks of school from the first day to the last day," she reported.

"Are those 41 weeks all teaching weeks?"

Lisa was surprised to hear that question. The truth was, they weren't all teaching weeks. "Actually, they're not." She explained that, although some teaching occurred, most of the first week of school was used for setting expectations and getting acquainted. Similarly, the last week of school was spent giving and grading exams and preparing report cards. There was one week in the spring that was pretty much eaten up with standardized testing, and another week in the fall when the entire seventh grade was away at environmental camp. And then there is one whole week off over Christmas break and the week of spring vacation. "So, no, not all of those 41 weeks are teaching weeks."

"We need to zero in on the actual number of teaching weeks you have to work with on which to develop the load leveling plan. Rule those lost weeks out of the mix. Of the weeks left, are there any partial weeks?"

Lisa knew she had some of those as well. Conference weeks only had three teaching days, as did Thanksgiving and teachers' convention weeks. She made sure those days were marked in her planner and tallied the final count. There were 23 full weeks of five teaching days and 11 weeks that had less than five days of teaching after eliminating the first and last week of school from consideration since they didn't include content teaching. "So, I would say I really only have 34 weeks available to teach, but remember, that number includes 11 short weeks."

"Are there any possibilities for other class-time losses?" Bill asked.

"Yes. Sometimes special programs or events are scheduled that invade your teaching time, but you can't anticipate those at the beginning of the year. And then there are the mandatory fire and tornado drills that take class time, but teachers don't usually get word on those until the day before or the day of the drill. You can't build them into a teaching plan, if that is what you are asking." Bill jotted notes down as Lisa continued to talk. "At first glance, these interruptions seem unimportant, but I was so frustrated this past year that I kept a log of how much time all these planned and unplanned interruptions took away from my classroom time. I lost over 120 hours of instructional time over the year, Bill! That's the equivalent of almost 15 days of class!"

"Then we're also going to need to build in slop time to ensure that you have enough time in spite of the interruptions," observed Bill. "So here's what I see, Lisa. You have 34 teaching weeks. If you build in two weeks of catch-up time for unanticipated interruptions, that leaves you with 32 teaching weeks over which you can build your load leveling plan. Do you follow how I got that figure?"

"Yes. I like the idea of building in the catch-up time."

"Now let's look at the book. What do you feel would be the best way to break it up into the 32 available segments?" asked Bill.

Lisa turned to the Table of Contents in the World Geography text and started to read off the titles, country after country. "I guess the best approach would be to try to divide the content into regions of adjacent and similar countries."

"That's a very reasonable approach. How many country groupings would that entail?"

Lisa continued to study the Table of Contents, briefly recalling the amount of material associated with each country. "I don't know offhand. It would depend on the commonalities or relationship I'd establish for each country to others in a given grouping. It could also depend on the level of importance I'd assign to that country or area. I think a grouping could range from one country to maybe a dozen. But I would have to figure out how many total groupings that would equal."

"Well, that's your next step, Lisa. I'll let you work on it for a few days. You're the expert at this. My only suggestion is to make a first-cut list of reasonable groupings. Then set it aside overnight. The next day, go back through it, at least twice. Ask yourself whether the groupings are in the most logical order. Could they be combined differently or realigned? Remember, to meet your takt time you have to be able to teach your grouping in a week. And you have a total of 32 groupings to be made. Once you feel you have your doable groupings ready, call me."

Bill noted the worried look on his academic friend's face. "You are making great progress, Lisa," Bill reassured her. "This up-front work is the hardest part. Just think carefully and don't labor too much over whether you made the right decision or not. We have plenty of time to reevaluate and change decisions. Right now your task is to get a first draft of your groupings. Fine tuning will come later."

Bill departed with a wave and a final encouragement of "You can do it!" while Lisa continued to pore over the textbook, flipping back and forth between sections. Potential country groupings surfaced in her mind as she evaluated various possibilities, and before she knew it, several hours had passed. *I think I'll wait until tomorrow to start developing the initial list,* she thought. She needed time to think more about all the things she and Bill had discussed earlier in the afternoon. *I need to revisit the learning theory concepts and be sure I include them in my decision making,* she concluded as she locked her classroom door and walked down the hall.

The next morning, Lisa eagerly dove into the development of her plan. She recalled Bill's outline of her task: focus on getting an initial list of 32 reasonable groupings, each of which could be taught in a week. *And some of those weeks,* she reminded herself, *will end up being less than five days, but I'm not going to worry about that now.* Basing some of her decisions on her previous experience teaching the course, Lisa started fleshing out a weekly curriculum scope. She found herself working in a logical sequence modeled somewhat after the sequence of the text, but remembered that Bill had said sequence should not be the primary concern at this stage.

I'm still going to start with the United States and Canada, she thought. *That area is most relevant to the students. Then I'll move south to teach Mexico, Central America, and South America. The traditions, cultures, language, and natural resources of these countries have so many similarities.* She struggled with the number of countries to group together in South America, but kept to the strategy of making a first cut. *I need to wait and see how many groupings come out of this initial attempt,* she reminded herself. *Wouldn't it be awesome if that number turned out to be 32?!*

The Americas proved to be a breeze compared to Europe, the continent Lisa tackled next. She decided she did not want to take a "popcorn" approach, teaching first one country here and then another country there. *The students need a pattern to follow, a sequence that provides a basis for understanding.* Examining a directional approach, Lisa first evaluated a north to south sequence, then an east to west sequence. Using one of her European outline map masters, she circled potential groupings in Europe with various colored pencils before going on to Asia, Asia Minor, and the Middle East. And to prevent herself from influencing her first-pass decisions based on the limit of 32, she purposely did not number the groupings as she made them.

Over the next several hours Lisa progressed through the decision-making process, fiercely debating with herself on multiple occasions. *How can I devote an entire week to the study of Israel when so many other countries warrant in-depth study as well? How can I not when the Middle East crisis has influenced so many actions and reactions within today's global society?! My students need to understand the basis of the conflict!* Some decisions were much less controversial. As she worked further around the globe, Lisa found her decision-making process becoming less daunting. Finally, she attacked Australia, Oceania, and Antarctica, which collectively provided an easy conclusion to the entire first-pass planning endeavor.

Lisa stood up and stretched. Her back was stiff from sitting in the hunched position she had been in for hours. She tilted her head from side to side, and walked around her work table as she gazed at the list. *I wonder what the total is?* she thought. *Not gonna look at that yet,* she decided. *I should review it one time first and make sure I'm happy with these group-ings as they are. But I need to get away from this for a bit.* She was sur-prised when she looked at the clock on the wall to find it was already 2 PM. *No wonder I'm hungry!*

To take a mental break and get some food, Lisa left school, stopped to pick up a sandwich, and then forced herself to eat her late lunch at a local park where she could be outdoors in the fresh air. Before she got back in her car, she took a short walk. Moving always helped her think more clearly, and walking energized her. She was eager and ready to get back to her task and determined that she would finish the first pass before she quit for the day.

Back in her classroom, Lisa sat down again at the work table to review what she had completed during her long morning. For the most part, she was pleased with the associations she had created, with a few exceptions. She considered realignment. Some she changed; others she returned to their former groupings. At long last she felt comfortable with the list. *Now to find out the total number of groups.*

Hoping against hope that somehow, magically, the resulting number would be exactly 32, Lisa began assigning numbers to the individual groups on her list. Her heart dropped as she wrote down the number 30 and there were many more groups to go. The total ended at 39. She had seven groups too many.

It was time to call her mentor.

"Hello, Bill. I just got done with the first pass. No, actually it's the second. I did the second after I went out for lunch and got away, as you sug-gested. I'm a little discouraged, although I'm sure you're going to tell me I shouldn't be. I came up with 39 groupings, not 32."

Bill was surprised to hear from Lisa so soon. "Well, you're right about my reaction, Lisa, because I am going to tell you not to be discouraged. Did you really think you'd get 32 on your first attempt?"

"I guess not, Bill," she admitted begrudgingly, "but I sure had my fingers crossed."

Bill laughed on the other end. "It never happens that way. What you have experienced is normal. In fact, you actually got closer than I would have predicted for the first pass. But seven isn't insurmountable."

"Seven is huge, Bill! How am I going to essentially massage seven groups away?!" Bill took notice of the desperation in Lisa's voice as well as her choice of words.

"I understand your concern and worry," he began calmly, "but this is precisely why I told you that you need to walk away from your first pass at least overnight. You've spent the better part of your day thinking on this, and frankly, Lisa, your brain is fried! Go home, go shopping, go see a movie, go rollerblading—do whatever you want, but do not think about this any more today. You need to refresh your brain for your second pass tomorrow."

"Bill, honestly, I don't think I can take *seven* groups out!" Lisa blurted.

"I hear what you are saying, Lisa. But I need you to do what I'm telling you to do and trust me that it's the right thing. You need to physically get away from this for the rest of the day, and that means you're not to think about it, either. Clear your mind and do something active. You need to give it overnight before you begin a second pass or you won't be able to see possible solutions. Right now you are mentally stuck on the number seven. Tomorrow, you won't be. You will be open to seeing a new perspective. You'll see your groupings in a new light. And you will find solutions as well as more problems."

"More problems?!"

"Well, actually it would be more accurate to say you won't be as happy with some of the grouping decisions you made today when you look at them tomorrow."

"Oh, no!"

"Lisa, you need to trust me on this. You did a great job on this first pass. Tomorrow you will be enlightened and see how to reach your goal much more clearly than you do right now. This is just how continuous improvement works."

Whether it was Bill's permission to quit for the day or her own relief at not having to think any more on the problem for the rest of the day, Lisa agreed to follow Bill's recommendation. She hung up the phone after thanking her mentor for his counsel and repeating aloud his directive for the next day: start at the end and work backwards to gain a different perspective, and expect enlightenment to set in.

ZEROING IN

The next day, Lisa spread out her list and the outline map masters that showed the preliminary groupings she had created the day before. Making a quick visual assessment, she was satisfied that every country was incorporated into her plan. She also noted a natural flow to the sequence of the countries as they were introduced. *I'm going to try to preserve that flow*, she decided. The question was how to accomplish that when she had to make changes.

I think I'm going to approach this by seeing if I can absorb peripheral countries from some groups into adjacent groups, she thought to herself. *Hopefully, Bill's advice to review the groups in reverse order will help me see how to make the changes as well as keep this flow.* She numbered a piece of scratch paper from 1 to 7, intending to mark off each excess group as she reassigned its countries. Finally ready to tackle the second pass, Lisa turned her attention to the last set of countries she had identified the day before: Australia, New Zealand, Oceania, and Antarctica.

Bill had predicted that the new perspective gained by an end-to-beginning review would reveal new insight, and Lisa immediately found that to be true. *What was I thinking?!* she asked herself as she contemplated teaching those four areas in one week. *Those areas should be in three separate groups!* Bill wasn't kidding when he said she might not be happy today with the groups she formed yesterday, and that this could cause problems. "Hey, Lisa," she reminded herself out loud, "you're supposed to be reducing the number of groups, not adding more!"

Working backwards through Asia, Lisa shifted countries into similar but somewhat different groupings, justifying each new orientation with a logical rationale and ensuring that it could be taught in a week. For several hours she seesawed through possible options, adopting new groupings and rejecting others. Some groups she left untouched.

With the first reassignment of a complete group, Lisa crossed off the number seven on her checkoff sheet. *Only six to go!* Slowly but steadily she whittled the numbers down, one by one. By the time she finished her reevaluation of Asia and Europe, Lisa had reduced the number of groups by five. She eliminated the sixth by recombining groups in South America, and cut the seventh by combining the geography of Canada and the United States. *I can justify that,* she explained to herself, *because students would have already had U.S. geography as part of their U.S. History studies in fifth grade. We won't be starting from scratch there.*

A real sense of accomplishment brought a smile to Lisa's face as she crossed off the last of the seven numbers that represented the challenge of the second pass. She glanced at the clock. Another day and lunch time had flown by. One more time she read over the new weekly curriculum plan she had just finished. She was happy with the results—32 doable groupings. *But could those that fell sequentially in a short week be completed in less than five days?* Deciding that evaluation was a project for a new day, Lisa tucked the updated list of groups in her planner and set it on the work table, determined to take up that challenge the next day.

"Bill," she reported later that evening by phone, "I was able to get the groupings down to 32."

"That's great! Was it as difficult as you thought it was going to be?"

"Actually, I'm surprised by how difficult it wasn't. I would have preferred not having to go through the process a second time, but looking back, I think I would still be deliberating over the first pass if I'd had to focus on getting the groups right the first time. It's kind of like writing a paper. The hardest part is doing that first draft and getting things down. The second and additional drafts are cleanup efforts."

"*Drafts* is a perfect description of what you are creating here. And there will be more."

"I know. I have 32 groups, but I'm not sure all of them can be done in partial weeks. Nor do I know which groups will fall in full or partial weeks. So my plan for tomorrow is to lay the sequence of groups out in the planner and see how they line up with the calendar. I may still have to make some adjustments."

"To your groups?" asked Bill.

"No," Lisa responded. She had already thought that through and developed an action plan for the next day. "I want to preserve the groupings I have now and as much as possible the sequence flow from one group to another. What I'm going to evaluate for tomorrow is whether I may need to flip-flop a grouping from one week to the next or adjust activities within a week."

"Lisa, you are living proof that implementing lean continuous improvement is pure common sense!"

"What do you mean?"

"You have just informed me that flow is integral to teaching and your students' learning. Streamlining flow is one of the core principles of lean. So you are already incorporating that into your design without me even pointing it out. The second thing is that your plan for tomorrow is essentially, as I understand it, to make sure that what you need to teach in each week can fit into the teaching time available that week. Is that correct?"

"Yes."

Bill's voice belied his pleasure. "Lisa, what you are planning for tomorrow falls under another lean technique we call mistake-proofing."

"What?"

"When an action is taken that will prevent a mistake from being made in the future, that's mistake-proofing. Your calendar check tomorrow is a form of mistake-proofing because it will prevent you and your students from taking on more curriculum in a given week than you can successfully handle. You are a natural born lean practitioner, Lisa! You are doing a great job! Your plan for tomorrow is excellent. Good luck, and call me when you've finalized your sequencing."

A surge of excitement raced through Lisa as she pulled into the school parking lot the next morning. Added to her satisfaction at finalizing the country groups the day before were her high hopes for completing the curriculum calendar by the end of the day. That was the goal she had set for herself, and she was determined to meet it. *I think it would be a good idea to document the textbook pages each grouping covers as I assign them to a calendar week,* she decided as she walked down the corridor to her room. *I want this plan to be very visual for me as well as for Bill when he reviews it. If something isn't going to work, I want it to stand out like a sore thumb!*

Lisa's success at meeting Bill's first challenge in designing the load leveling plan motivated her efforts that morning, and her enthusiasm grew during the day. Following the sequence she had finalized the day before, Lisa assigned the country groups in her preferred order to consecutive weeks in her planner, starting at the beginning of the school year. As she entered each group, she also recorded the corresponding pages in the textbook (see Figure 1). When that task was done, she went back for a second pass to look specifically at the 11 short weeks. *Can I complete the assigned curriculum for those weeks in the available teaching time?* The biggest worries were the three-day weeks. But Lisa found that she only needed to adjust her sequence twice to reassign longer curriculum segments that had randomly

Week of	Country(s) to be covered	Pages in the text
Sept 8–11	First week of school	
Sept 14–18	Review map skills and pretest	
Sept 21–25	Review geography themes, color maps	
Sept 28–Oct 2	United States and Canada	89–131
Oct 5–9	Mexico and Central America	153–183
Oct 12–16	West Indies	183–193
Oct 19–23	Brazil and its neighbors	195–210
Oct 26–30	Andes countries	217–232
Nov 2–6	British Isles and Scandinavia	255–270
Nov 9–13	France, Germany, Benelux, and Alpine countries	277–293
Nov 16–20	Portugal, Spain, Italy, and Greece	297–313
Nov 23–27 TKSG	Czech Republic, Slovakia, the Balkans	332–338
Nov 30–Dec 4	Baltic republics, Poland, Hungary	319–331
Dec 7–11	Russia and independent lands	348–376
Dec 14–18	Catch-up week	
Dec 21–Jan 1	Christmas break	No school
Jan 4–8	Independent, Caucasus, Central Asia republics	383–399
Jan 11–15	SW Asia, Turkey, Lebanon, Syria, Jordan	408–430
Jan 18–22	Arabian peninsula, Iran, Iraq, Afghanistan	431–438
Jan 25–29	Israel	423–427
Feb 1–5	Exodus—the film / Catch-up week	
Feb 8–12	Middle East discussions	
Feb 15–19	North Africa, the Sahel countries	444–461; 470–473; 490–493
Feb 22–26	Nigeria and the coastal countries	484–489; 494–501
Mar 1–5	East Africa	521–538
Mar 8–12	Central Africa	505–517
Mar 15–19	Spring break	
Mar 22–26	Environmental Camp	No classes
Mar 29–Apr 2	Antarctica	718–723
Apr 5–9	South Africa	545–564
Apr 12–16	South Asia, subcontinent	574–598
Apr 19–23	Himalayan and island countries	599–602
Apr 26–30	China	609–626
May 3–7	Japan and the Koreas	633–648
May 10–14	Mainland SE Asia, 7 Islands	655–668
May 17–21	New Zealand and Oceania	678–692
May 24–28	Australia	703–723
May 31–Jun 4	Wrap-up week—Geography Bee?? Celebrate doing the entire curriculum!!!???	

Figure 1   Lisa's country groupings with corresponding pages in the textbook.

fallen to three-day weeks, and flip-flopped them with short West Indies and Antarctica segments. She decided not to make any changes to four-day weeks until she talked with Bill.

"This doesn't look too bad," Lisa commented aloud as she reviewed the second-pass effort she had completed. "If we can keep to this schedule, there might even be time to do some additional fun things on catch-up weeks and at the end of the year." And then, all of a sudden, a glaring omission in her planning jumped off the page, and Lisa's heart sank.

"Oh no! I haven't built in any time for midterms or final exams!" Upon further examination, Lisa also realized she had not scheduled time for student presentations on the special project she assigned in the first term. Refusing to panic, Lisa reminded herself that she was to call Bill when she had concluded her sequencing. *Hopefully, he will have an idea to address this problem besides going back to the drawing board.*

ESTABLISHING "STANDARD WORK"

The next day, Bill arrived eager to see the results of Lisa's sequencing. He was impressed with the thoroughness of her layout. Bill even noted the out-of-sequencing that occurred to allow for short weeks. "Very good," he complimented his protégé. "How do you feel about it?"

"The layout I like, Bill, but I realized last night that I did not build in time to evaluate learning. As you can see there are no midterm or final tests listed."

"Are you required to give them?"

"Well, it's common practice to give them. Virtually everyone does."

"But are you required to give them, Lisa?" Bill asked once again.

"Technically, I guess not. But periodic assessments have to be done to make sure the kids are learning. Those assessments also provide data for a report card."

"Hmm." Bill contemplated the problem. "What if you did weekly quality checks instead?"

"Quality checks? What is that?"

"Well, it seems to me your assessments are simply what we call a quality check, Lisa, a check on the quality of the learning taking place. Isn't that the goal of the assessments you give?"

"Yes, it is. The tests determine whether learning has taken place, and if it hasn't, then I need to reteach the material so the student can master it."

"Well, then why would you wait so long between assessments to determine whether quality learning has taken place? Wouldn't it make more sense to do a weekly quality check after your week's curriculum has been delivered than to wait several weeks to identify and remedy a problem after you've gone on to other areas of study?"

Bill's comment made perfect sense to Lisa. Weekly assessments would allow for rapid-response problem identification and intervention. It would provide her with more data on learning, which, she believed, would make possible a more accurate overall assessment. She would also be able to provide both students and parents with real-time performance information when they asked for it. And weekly assessments should discourage procrastination by the students. The more she thought about the idea of testing weekly, the more benefits she could see in choosing that course of action.

"Bill, that's a brilliant idea for so many reasons. Not only will weekly tests allow me to keep better track of how the kids are doing and provide remediation in a timely fashion if needed, they actually seem more aligned with learning as a continuous effort. If I test every week, I could actually recycle some old test questions and keep the learning fresh and ongoing."

"Ah yes, adding to those ten impressions for mastery learning, are you?"

"Omigosh! I hadn't even thought of that"—Lisa's excitement was obvious—"but recycling questions from previously learned material definitely would extend the number of impressions! Oh yeah! I'm definitely doing your weekly quality checks!" Lisa said with conviction. "I won't be giving my students permission to forget!"

Bill delighted in her enthusiasm. "I can honestly say that I have never seen anyone so excited about a quality check."

Lisa laughed aloud. "There's a selfish component to my excitement, Bill. Besides the fact that this plan will be better for the students and their learning, it's actually solved my scheduling problem. I don't have to redo the scheduling plan! If I'm going to make every Friday the assessment day for that week's curriculum, and I'm including questions from the whole term, I don't need midterm or final exams!"

Bill held his hand out to shake Lisa's. "Congratulations, Lisa! I would call your plan continuous improvement in action. And you know what? There is a similar approach called Training Within Industry (TWI) that has successfully employed the same strategies you are describing to teach work skills to people. Your strategy already has a track record of success!"

Lisa could not contain her exuberance. She could see the components of her load leveling plan coming together in the way she anticipated would enable her to deliver her entire curriculum. Additionally, she could also see *un*anticipated benefits that would enhance and keep student learning moving forward.

"I'm really excited about this. This will be a more efficient and effective way to teach and learn, don't you think?"

"I do, indeed!" agreed Bill.

Lisa tried to bring herself back down to earth. "So, what do we do next?" she asked.

Bill replied with a question of his own. "What would you normally do next?"

The educator spoke with the confidence that comes from familiarity with a process. "I would start laying out exactly how to deliver the weekly curriculum. I need to flesh out what I need to cover and, more importantly, how I'm going to cover it. I have to build in those ten impressions per week. And I need to look for and refine that teaching delivery pattern we talked about before."

"Sounds like another round of decision making, Lisa, but this time on patterns and methodologies," Bill remarked. "Let me ask some questions to help me understand what you feel you have to accomplish and why. And if some of my questions seem odd, remember, teaching is your area of expertise, not mine."

"OK, Bill, ask away."

"We talked before about general things you do to teach a unit. But can you tell me in more specific detail what you have normally done in the past to teach a unit?"

Lisa was a little confused by Bill's question. "I'm not sure I know what you mean."

"What specific activities do you do?"

"Well, normally I would go over the appropriate sections in the textbook, and depending on the unit, use other materials, and lecture on important points that aren't in the text. I always have the kids take notes to build listening and evaluation skills. They read current events articles and other pertinent readings. And I also have them create a topographical map—no geography course can be complete without doing maps so students can visualize the land and then tie it to the lecture points. We might view part of a video, have a visit by a guest speaker, or go on field trips. I often challenge the students on a dilemma that might be happening in that geographic area. And to round out their experience, I'd like them to be exposed to music, artifacts, crafts, and even food from the regions we study, if I can work those things in."

Bill could see a major challenge looming for Lisa. "If what you just described is part of each unit's learning, and you are redesigning your units to be a week long, I guess the next question is, Can you fit all of those activities in a week?"

The answer was obvious to Lisa. "No."

Bill nodded his head in agreement with her assessment. "So what you are going to have to decide next is what you believe you can reasonably fit in a week's instructional time."

The teacher stared at her mentor, speechless. Where would she even start in paring down those activities?

Now Bill felt the need for his coaching to begin in earnest. "When approaching a significant challenge like this, Lisa, you need to remind yourself of the basic focus of lean: identify and eliminate whatever is unnecessary or does not add value. Of everything you just described to me as something you routinely do, ask yourself: what is necessary to learn the curriculum, what is unnecessary, what adds value to student learning, and what doesn't? That's your starting framework for decision making. Remember, this is all about learning to tackle problems by thinking about them differently."

With Bill's encouragement, Lisa listed on her whiteboard all of the learning activities she had previously identified. Then she described what each activity consisted of and what she felt it added to student understanding. She believed that every activity added value to a certain degree because student learning was enriched by each. But, she acknowledged after further questioning from Bill, some activities had greater value than others in facilitating the basic learning that was the goal of the course. "I do realize this is an introductory course in World Geography, not a graduate-level course," she admitted during their discussion.

Bill guided Lisa in the construction and use of a decision matrix, a lean tool that he assured her would make the decision-making process easier by making it visual. Using the matrix, Lisa was able to weight the contribution of each activity and quickly identify the critical components that would fit into her teaching week (see Figure 2).

"This is really slick, Bill! I can combine the important information from the text and the resource materials in a presentation, have the kids take notes, limit assignments to the production of a topographical map, and then use one day for discussion or extension activities."

"So, if I understand you correctly, there would be three basic elements in your standard teaching week—a presentation element, a map element, and, for lack of a better term, an enrichment element that would involve a pertinent class discussion. Would that be correct?"

"Yes, but I also assign a special project at the beginning of each term that everyone has to do. I have always taken time each week to monitor their progress and address any problems they might have encountered. I think that monitoring activity is important to include somehow." Lisa

Key: High = 3 Medium = 2 Low = 1	Essential for foundation learning	Student interest/fun	Feasible weekly	Enrichment contribution	Promotes lasting impression	Total
Go over text	2	1	2	1	1	7
Lecture	3	2	3	2	2	12
Dilemma discussion	1	3	3	2	2	11
Other materials/resources	2	2	3	2	2	11
Note taking	3	1	3	1	3	11
Outside readings	1	2	3	2	1	9
Current events	1	1	3	1	1	7
Topographical map	3	1	2	3	3	12
Videos/clips	1	3	1	2	2	9
Guest speaker	1	2	1	2	2	8
Field trip	1	3	1	2	2	9
Music	1	3	3	1	1	9
Examine artifacts	2	3	3	3	3	14
Try crafts	1	3	1	2	1	8
Sample food	1	3	1	1	2	9
Project checkpoint	2	1	3	2	3	11
Game	1	3	3	2	2	11
Review	3	2	3	3	3	14
Assessment	3	1	3	1	3	11

Figure 2   Lisa's decision matrix for weighting classroom activities.

watched as Bill recorded on the whiteboard the important elements she had identified.

"How much time have you taken for that activity in the past?" Bill asked.

Lisa shrugged her shoulders. "Really, not much. I check to make sure the students are on track and help them with their project management, and then we share or brainstorm resource options when someone gets stuck in their research. It probably takes me ten minutes to do the checkpoint and maybe five to seven minutes for the resource sharing."

"OK, let me jot that down here," Bill said as he added the checkpoint to his list. "It might be a factor we may need to address when you finalize your standard week. Is there anything else that you think is essential?"

"Well, this isn't technically essential from the curriculum standpoint, but I believe that students learn more when they are having fun, so I have used games to motivate and encourage self-directed learning. For this class I've incorporated my own version of Carmen Sandiego, giving clues that the kids research and decipher to identify Carmen's location each week. It's kind of a fun challenge, which they like, but I don't grade it. They compete for a prize. I think that pretty much sums up what I've incorporated into the class."

Bill added the Carmen Sandiego game to the list, then stepped back to review it with Lisa. "So it looks like there are four, maybe five things. What about the assessment piece you spoke of? Are you still planning to do that weekly?"

"Oh yes!" Lisa replied. "We need to add that in because an assessment will definitely be a part of each week."

Bill stepped forward and added Lisa's last component to the whiteboard, then turned to face her. "All right. What you see listed here are the components you have identified as essential parts of your standard week. So your next step will be . . ."

Lisa interrupted her teacher. "Bill, you keep saying 'standard week.' What does that mean?"

"Sorry, Lisa," Bill smiled as he apologized, "you're doing so well that I've forgotten you are new to lean!" He went on. "In lean, it is desirable to establish standard work. *Standard work* is defined as the routinely accepted set sequence of activities needed to accomplish a given task. It's what is done, and the order in which it is done, to complete a task. From my perspective, your standard work will be the sequence of learning activities that you decide on to deliver your course curriculum to your students. It's the routine you establish for your teaching. And since you have decided that your teaching cycle, or takt time, is a week, your standard work will be completed in a standard workweek, which I've taken the liberty of abbreviating to the term *standard week*. Does that make sense?"

"I guess what I think I'm hearing you say is that what I will determine as my routine in delivering the curriculum each week is what you are calling my standard work. Is that right?"

"Yes!"

"Bill, I don't want to offend you, but why is it so important to have standard work as long as I do what I need to get done?"

"Great question!" Bill complimented Lisa. "You have to have a standard *for* your work before you can make improvements to that work. Think about it, Lisa, an improvement is doing something better than it was done before, right? Well, how will you know if something is better if there is nothing to measure the new way against, a standard to compare the new way to? What you are going to do first is set your standard that you will measure everything in the future against—the routine of work you establish as your starting point in improving your teaching process. That starting point will be your standard until you change your routine, and when you implement that change the new routine will become the standard that you will measure the next new way against. Get it?"

Lisa was still somewhat confused. "Okay, so you are calling the old way something is done the standard way. But what does that have to do with what I teach? The curriculum will be different every week."

Patiently, Bill continued to clarify the concept. "Yes, your subject matter will be different each week, but how you do it will have the same pattern. Remember our earlier conversation in which we discussed how people learn and work in patterns? You were surprised to discover there was a pattern to the way you teach and the activities you use to deliver your curriculum. Look here"—Bill went back to the whiteboard and pointed to the list of five elements Lisa had identified as essential to her teaching the World Geography course—"you've already pointed out that you need to do these five basic activities. Those are the components of your standard work each week. What you have to determine now is whether they can be done in the same sequence each week. If they can, you will have defined the two necessary requirements that make up your standard work: substance and sequence."

"So if I do the same activities in the same order each week, that defines my standard work in a week or, as you refer to it, my standard work week?"

Bill smiled in concurrence as he nodded.

Enlightenment lit up Lisa's face. "I get it now. Then the key is to have the same pattern of activities in the task of teaching a unit." That realization acted as a catalyst for further understanding. "That even fits the brain and learning theory models, Bill. But what about the improvement part?"

"We have to set the standard before improvements can be made, Lisa. I want you to focus on creating your standard routine for a week. That will help you manage your teaching processes to ensure that all the required work gets done in the time allotted, and that is crucial to doing load leveling successfully. So your next challenge is to take this list of essential elements and develop a logical sequence and schedule in which to deliver them in a week's time."

"That reminds me of another problem I wanted to talk with you about."

"What's that?"

Lisa described her concern from the previous day. She would make her plan for five-day instructional weeks. She knew she would have to severely restrict activities for the several three-day weeks within the calendar. But she wasn't sure how to deal with the four-day weeks.

"I don't have the answer to that, Lisa, but you will as you design your instructional pattern. Just make sure the absolutely essential activities can be done in your shortest time period of three days and that you do them first to ensure they get done. Use the additional day or days to add the enrichment. At least that's what I'd do. But as I said, the answer will come to you as you think through your schedule and sequence design. I guarantee it."

Lisa ran her fingers through her hair, already beginning to evaluate possible options. Bill continued with his encouragement. "Draw yourself five columns on the whiteboard. Fill in the essential activities in the first two. Put your assessment in the third. If you can get those basic essential activities to fit into two days and assess on the third, you are in good shape. Then, depending on whether your week is four or five days, you can add the not necessary but value-adding activities as the number of days in the week allows. That way you can plan for three-, four-, or five-day weeks just by expanding on your basic set sequence. Does that make sense?"

Lisa stared at the whiteboard while nodding. "I think so. Absolutely necessary activities, including the assessment, have to fit in three days to ensure that the pattern will work for the short three-day week. Then I need to figure out what the pattern would be if I have a four-day week, and another pattern if I have a five-day week."

"You have this locked down tighter than a drum! Take the time to think this through carefully, and then let's get together when you're comfortable with your pattern and sequence. I'll wait to hear from you."

FLESHING OUT THE DETAILS

With a fifty-five-minute class period, it was obvious to Lisa that covering the vital material of her new week-long units would have to be accomplished via lecture. She was sure that was the only way to control time usage and ensure that she covered everything. The fact of the matter was that she couldn't count on students to read the text on their own time, and there simply wasn't time within two class periods to read through the text and use resource materials, too. Her best option to guarantee that students got the information she deemed necessary was to give it to them herself, which meant, she realized, that she would have to condense the material from the text and other resources and incorporate it into a lecture. It would be work for her to develop new lecture notes, but this would be part of that up-front effort Bill had described. The time she would invest in creating those notes that first year, she told herself, would pay dividends in subsequent years when she could reuse them.

Now mentally committed to operating on Bill's concept of a standard week, Lisa found herself trying to figure out what it would look like and how to optimize its design for student learning.

If I give the kids the critical information in a short three-day week, I have to make sure I can give it in its entirety in one day. We need to review it the second day so they can test on it the third day. So the shortest weeks really have to be limited in scope. Lisa went back through her planner and satisfied herself that the units she had assigned to the three-day weeks were short enough to cover in a single day. She felt they were.

For four-day weeks she would take two full days to present material, she decided. A third day would be used for the review. And the fourth would be for the assessment (see Figure 3). If there were five days, the extra day could be used for an additional value-adding activity, but which one? The choices from her list were: time for creating the assigned topographical map, a video clip, a guest speaker, discussion, the project check, artifact examination, a game, readings, field trip, listening to music, ethnic crafts,

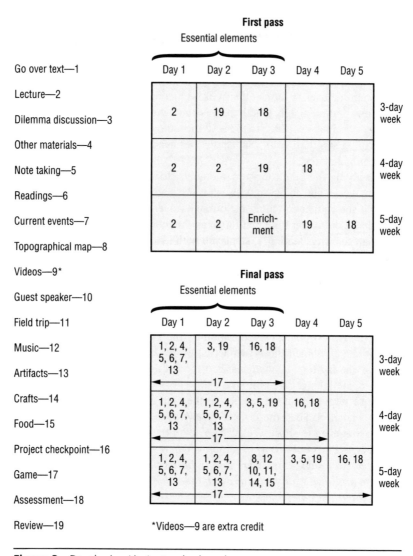

Go over text—1

Lecture—2

Dilemma discussion—3

Other materials—4

Note taking—5

Readings—6

Current events—7

Topographical map—8

Videos—9*

Guest speaker—10

Field trip—11

Music—12

Artifacts—13

Crafts—14

Food—15

Project checkpoint—16

Game—17

Assessment—18

Review—19

First pass

Essential elements

	Day 1	Day 2	Day 3	Day 4	Day 5	
	2	19	18			3-day week
	2	2	19	18		4-day week
	2	2	Enrich-ment	19	18	5-day week

Final pass

Essential elements

	Day 1	Day 2	Day 3	Day 4	Day 5	
	1, 2, 4, 5, 6, 7, 13	3, 19	16, 18			3-day week
	1, 2, 4, 5, 6, 7, 13	1, 2, 4, 5, 6, 7, 13	3, 5, 19	16, 18		4-day week
	1, 2, 4, 5, 6, 7, 13	1, 2, 4, 5, 6, 7, 13	8, 12 10, 11, 14, 15	3, 5, 19	16, 18	5-day week

←————— 17 —————→

*Videos—9 are extra credit

Figure 3 Developing Lisa's standard work.

or sampling food. Of those options, Lisa felt discussion had the greatest potential for expanding student understanding.

"Here comes the first pass for the standard work," she said aloud as she picked up a marker and started mapping a teaching routine. The routine would be a function of the number of available teaching days during a particular week. The first day of every week would be lecture. The last day of every week would be the assessment day. Between lecture and assessment had to be a day for review. *There was the standard for a three-day teaching week right there*, Lisa noted. A four-day week would include a second day of lecture on the second day of class, followed by the review day, and conclude with the assessment day. A five-day week would follow the routine for a four-day week, with a discussion day thrown in on Wednesday.

Stepping back to look at the weekly calendar she had just created, Lisa recognized immediately that there was an identifiable routine to this plan as well as a defined sequence to the activities, the two elements Bill described as defining standard work. She shook her head almost in disbelief at how easily it had materialized.

Studying the plan for a few moments, Lisa was pleased with the initial sequence, but unhappy with what she had had to abandon. She wondered if she could combine some of the leftovers with what she had already included. Letting her imagination go as she looked from the list to the five-day plan she was creating, Lisa played with ideas. What if she incorporated introduction of artifacts and their examination into the lecture component? That could easily be done, she decided. It wouldn't be difficult to combine a discussion and a review in one class period, providing half the time for each activity. After all, twenty-five minutes was a decent amount of time in which to discuss a topic, and the same amount of time would allow for a rapid-fire review game as preparation for the assessment the following day. And if she combined those two activities on the review day, that freed up the middle day for . . . she consulted the list again . . . the map work, she decided, and plugged that into the plan.

Lisa stepped back and reviewed the plan and the list once again. She really wanted to keep the project review time, too. How could she incorporate that even in short weeks? She noted that Bill had recorded that the time needed was only 10 to 15 minutes. *Where could that fit? Certainly not in the lecture days—they were totally full. Taking that time from the discussion and review day would lessen the value of those two activities. But what about the assessment day?* Lisa ran over in her mind what she did for the project check. She did a quantitative review of the students' project binders to make sure each person was on track for completion by the due date, and the students also had the opportunity to identify challenges in finding resources and share discovered resources with each other. *Wait a minute!* A brilliant idea came to her mind. *What if I did the quantitative check at the same time the kids were doing their test?* She asked herself. *I don't need to talk to them during that check. I only need to talk to someone if they are missing project components and I could do that at the end of class. If I design each week's test so it can be completed in 45 minutes, we can use the last ten minutes of the assessment day to do the research sharing! Yes!* She could see this was doable, and she was excited to keep that important value-adding component in her teaching plan. In fact, Lisa was feeling very pleased. Even in short three- and four-day weeks, she saw how she could include the majority of her value-adding activities. Possibilities leaped off the board at her. She could also run her Carmen Sandiego game, she decided, by continuing to do what she had always done, which was to post four different clues each week on her bulletin board and give the answer on the last day; she would just amortize the distribution of the clues over the non-assessment days of the week. She would make one change, though, and locate the focused destination of the game for the week in the area of each week's study rather than a randomly selected location. That way the game would not only make learning fun, it would also support and enhance the weekly curriculum. Lisa's satisfaction with her plan grew with each new adopted idea.

Returning her attention to the list, she was bothered that value-adding elements still weren't assigned. Lisa realized she didn't have time to do all of those activities every week, but she told herself, *I do have a good number of five-day weeks, and those would provide another day in which those activities could fit.* She decided that on the full weeks, she would follow the sequence of the first two days being lecture and the last two days being discussion/review and assessment. She had already decided to make the middle day for students to work on their maps, but felt they could do that while they listened to music from the region studied that week. Lisa decided she could also provide a periodic food sampling during this time, at the conclusion of a continent's study. And an occasional guest speaker could be invited on that day without losing any critical value-adding activities or time. Determined to find a way to recover as many components as she could, she even devised an extra credit opportunity for students who view the entire videos of which she would have shown brief clips! *I am going to have my cake and eat it, too!* she rejoiced.

WHAT IS A WEEK?

With her overall delivery plan sketched out, Lisa focused her next pass on building-in mastery learning components. Lisa had been studying brain and learning theories for years and had incorporated elements of these in her teaching up to this point. But because of the rigorous design of this class, she especially wanted to construct it in a way that included the ten impressions of information that research showed were needed to store information in long-term memory. She approached her next level of planning with that goal in mind.

"I'm going to focus on how to incorporate this in a four- or five-day week," she decided. The research findings she felt were important to her planning were:

- Ten impressions of the information had to be received by the learner.

- The impressions should, ideally, be delivered in different formats and modalities or combinations of modalities (visual, auditory, kinesthetic).

- The impressions must be separated in time.

- Learning is cemented during sleep periods.

- Each person has a preferred way of receiving information.

Lisa began exploring how many impressions she could create while following her newly identified standard work week format.

Lisa knew that she would have to do more than talk during her lecture time. Lisa knew she would initially present information verbally to her class, so her students' first impression would be an auditory one. She also knew that by using visual aids and her smart board, the students would also get visual impressions of that same information. She realized that she could build a kinesthetic impression into the lecture time if she provided artifacts for the students to examine and talk about, as well as have the students take notes. Taking notes was an activity that Lisa routinely incorporated in her classes to help students build active listening and evaluative skills. This would provide an impression in three different learning style formats in the one class. If the students read the textbook section covered that week, that would be another impression, but Lisa was realistic enough to know that few of her students actually read the text at all.

If she followed the same format over two days of presentation, Lisa would also create another impression in three modalities for the new material provided on the second day. The map work time on the third day would provide an additional impression using two modalities—a visual one looking at the map and a kinesthetic one in drawing the features. In-class review on the fourth day would provide yet another impression. Lisa calculated that nightly homework Monday through Thursday of reviewing the notes and map would provide four more impressions. Plus there was the assessment test itself, and going over each test question and its correct answer when the test was returned the following Monday would account for a grand total of ten potential impressions. She was confident her format would lead to mastery learning.

The next day, Lisa gathered all the materials she needed to develop her presentation notes. For the most part, the country notes were prepared, but they needed to be restructured to match the groupings she had chosen. Lisa also had to fine-tune her presentations to accommodate the new syllabus and her weekly unit structure. That meant presentations had to be completed on their scheduled days. For the most part, her current maps would work as is; she would combine some depending on the grouping size, but that was a simple matter of adding or subtracting countries to the outline master for each week. She reviewed her current list of dilemmas, evaluated them for continued relevance, and realigned them to match the topics with the weekly unit each supported.

Lisa next tackled her special projects. The first was a valuable assignment in her eyes, for multiple reasons. Not only did it facilitate in-depth learning about a country from the ethnic background of each student, it also taught students project management skills. The project itself had 24 components and was assigned over nine weeks. The first week was used to introduce, clarify, and provide basic resources for the project. At the end of the next eight weeks, Lisa conducted her checkpoint on the completion of three project components per week. She decided she would schedule student presentations of these projects during her first catch-up week, allowing a great deal of flexibility in time use. For her other special projects, Lisa decided to offer students the opportunity to view and review historical films of their choosing that dealt with geographical and cultural studies. This would work in another one of her left out value-adding activities and, she was sure, would provide the students with a broader understanding of the specific topic than the short movie clips she would have shown.

Methodically over the next weeks, Lisa tackled each component of her standard work. She pulled out the Carmen Sandiego clues from her recently reorganized files. She chuckled at how easy it was to locate everything she needed. Bill's 5S project, which didn't seem very relevant at the time they did it, certainly had proven a time-saver. There was no longer a need to search for anything. Spreading the target locations from the past year on her work table along with their respective clues, Lisa selected and assigned those that fit a particular unit, then picked new locations to fit the units without one. She completed the four clues for each new location with ease, made up clue cards, and replaced the now updated game folder in her filing cabinet.

The last task was to redesign the assessments as weekly tests. Lisa already had test questions and answers developed but needed to reformat them to match up with the weekly units. That complete rewrite took over a week. When she finished, Lisa reviewed the rework she had done and felt a real sense of satisfaction. Not only had she developed her plan, she was proud of herself for completing virtually all of the preparatory work she would need for the entire upcoming year! *It's unreal,* she commented to herself as she realized the full impact of the work she had accomplished in a few short weeks, *I have just made my job for the rest of the year so much easier! I'll actually have more time during the year because of the investment I've made in this pre-planning. Bill was absolutely right! In fact, it's time to call him and go on to whatever the next step is.*

THE REPORT-OUT

Two days later, Bill returned to the classroom. It had been nearly four weeks since he had done his last coaching there with Lisa. He was eager to see what his friend had accomplished, and Lisa was equally eager to share the progress she had made with her mentor.

"Well, the last time I was here," Bill recalled, "you had identified your weekly units and you were working on identifying your standard work. So fill me in on what you have done since then."

Lisa picked up her planner from the worktable. "You've seen this. It contains all the units assigned by week. I made sure that the few three-day weeks had unit topics that could be covered in that short period of time. That's verified and built into my teaching plan." She replaced the planner on the tabletop and stepped to the filing cabinet.

"Excellent," commented Bill, "that is actually a form of mistake-proofing, Lisa, and that step is a critical one in making your load leveling plan successful. You won't get off schedule in short weeks because you've built in the means to use them effectively."

Lisa opened the top two drawers of the filing cabinet. "These files contain the sequence of unit materials for the whole year, Bill. Each file has a complete set of presentation notes for the unit, an outline master for the topographical map for that week's assignment, with instructions for creating the map, a fully developed test and answer sheet for the unit, a dilemma question to be debated and discussed that is pertinent to the area we study that week, and a specific destination from the area and four clue cards for the Carmen Sandiego game."

Bill whistled in admiration. "Holy smokes! You really have been hustling! This is a very impressive accomplishment!"

"Oh that's not all, Bill," she went on proudly as she pointed across the room. "Over there in those labeled bins are the artifacts and CDs I'll be using each week in my presentations. It's all sorted by unit and in the sequence I'll be following." Lisa shut the two file drawers, then returned to the worktable. She pulled two papers from the front of her planner and handed them to her coach.

"The green sheet contains the syllabus for the entire year for this class. It shows what pages we will be covering in any given week, whether there will be a test and the date of the test, and what will be covered on the test. I plan to give the syllabus out to the kids during the first week of school as well as to the parents during open house. Everyone will know what we are doing and when we are doing it from day one."

"Great communication plan," Bill concurred as he reviewed the World Geography class syllabus. Everything was clearly noted on the spreadsheet, just as Lisa had described, and would be easy for both students and parents to follow.

"I know you'll be real interested in the yellow sheet. It outlines the standard work plan for the students and myself."

Bill eagerly studied the routine of work Lisa had defined.

"What you see here is the standard work for a five-day teaching week. Let me explain it to you, and then I will tell you how the standard work for four- and three-day weeks differs from this. We'll repeat this pattern of work each and every week." Lisa fleshed out her five-day plan as outlined in Figure 4.

Lisa explained that in four-day weeks there would be no map work time given in class. The map was, after all, the only routine homework product she would require of students. She felt they should be able to finish that assignment in four days working on it at home, and they would have forewarning in the syllabus whether they would have a class period to work on the map or not, so they could plan accordingly. The rest of the week would mirror the five-day week minus Wednesday: specifically, two days of presentation, a day for discussion and review, and a day for assessment and the project checkpoint. Three-day weeks would have one day of presentation, one day for discussion and review, and a day for assessment and the project checkpoint. Carmen Sandiego clues would be amortized over the week in such a way that the fourth clue would always be posted on the day before the test. Bill easily recognized the pattern as well as the standard work Lisa had defined: there were specific activities in a specific sequence (presentation, discussion and review, assessment). He congratulated her.

Monday

1. Give out week's materials to students:
   - Outline map master plus instructions for successfully completing it
   - Four world current event articles from the newspaper
   - The unit's dilemma question
   - Post the first of four Carmen Sandiego game clues, which will be posted daily thereafter
   - Reminders of any additional expectations (special assignment due dates)
2. Presentation on half of the unit's material
3. Clarify nightly homework expectations: read over notes and work on/review map
4. Give back and review previous week's assessment test
5. Students to take notes on lecture

Tuesday

1. Second half of presentation (Lisa explained that while there was a text, it was sadly lacking in dealing with modern issues and cultural information, which was an integral part of the course. She planned to use the text as a supplemental resource and the main source for maps. While the students were expected to read the assigned pages in the text, the main sources of information provided for each unit would be her multimedia presentations, examination of resources and artifacts, and any handouts she would provide.)
2. Post the next Carmen Sandiego clue
3. Homework assignment (see Monday)

Wednesday

1. Class time provided to finish maps while listening to and discussing the music of the nation or region; food tasting at conclusion of continental study; possible guest speaker from time to time
2. Post the next Carmen Sandiego clue
3. Homework assignment (see Monday)

Thursday

1. Discuss assigned unit dilemma
2. Review material from presentations
3. Post the next Carmen Sandiego clue
4. Homework assignment (see Monday)

Friday

1. Give Carmen Sandiego answer
2. Give assessment test
3. Special project checkpoint during test time
4. Resource sharing following test

Figure 4   Five-day plan.

"You should be very proud of this work, Lisa. I am certainly very proud of you! You have everything well mapped and supported—great organization. The plan ensures that you will cover the entire curriculum. But as I recall, completing the curriculum was just one of two big concerns you had. The other was student mastery. Does your plan address that concern?"

"That was on my mind throughout my planning, Bill," Lisa assured him. "You remember the lesson you had in brain and learning theories?"

Bill nodded. "I do, indeed. Everybody learns differently because we all have different learning styles, brains aren't designed to cram, people have to receive the information several times to learn it, and there has to be a period of time between study activities."

"You remembered that very well. Now I'm the one who is impressed! And, yes, all of that is incorporated into my plan. Let me tell you about that part because I am really excited about it." Lisa guided Bill's gaze down the yellow standard work sheet as she went on, pointing out various sections as she continued her explanation. "Over the course of the four- and five-day weeks there are at least ten opportunities for individual impressions to be made, the number of impressions that research says is necessary to get information into long-term memory." She outlined how various learning style modalities would be utilized on presentation days, how note taking, homework, review, and even test taking would contribute opportunities for the ten impressions. Furthermore, Lisa pointed out, students would be getting the impressions on a daily basis. "They will be getting a daily diet, so to speak. As you recall, brains are designed to handle small doses of information at a time, and we need to sleep on new information in order for it to be processed and stored as learning. Having the ten impressions fed over four days should significantly increase the chances that the information is stored in long-term memory because it is consistent with what research says brains need for effective memory retention. It all fits together and it's all self-supporting. If I can pull this off, I have a high level of confidence that we will finish the book, complete the curriculum, and achieve mastery learning. What do you think?"

The lean master laid the papers he had just reviewed down on the worktable, then lifted his eyes to meet those of his student. "I'm not a professional educator, Lisa, but to me this plan has a tremendous amount of merit. As a load-leveling plan, you have precisely planned the instructional scheduling to ensure complete delivery of your assigned curriculum, and this in spite of the problems you anticipate. You have even made provision for problems that you don't anticipate. You have built in multiple fail-safes. This is as good as load leveling gets. I do have a couple of devil's advocate questions to ask, but first I want to comment on this plan from a strictly lean perspective."

Bill went on. "As you know, lean focuses on the customer, adding value, and eliminating waste. Your plan does all of this.

"I see great emphasis on the customer at the whole school level. This project is purposely designed to ensure that you can provide *all* of the curriculum assigned to you by your customer, in this case your principal. The project demonstrates an understanding of the 13-year big picture as well as the domino effect on learning from incomplete curriculum delivery. Additionally, you have your students' parents as customers who will benefit from your plan since you will be maximizing the instruction they are paying for with their tax dollars. I am also very impressed with the focus you have given to your students as customers, Lisa. Not only does your plan provide the expanded opportunity for them to learn the complete course, your incorporation of all the brain and learning strategies is specifically designed to help each individual student learn better. That is true customer focus in my book.

"I do have one question pertaining to your impression strategy, though. Are you going to just use this knowledge in your instruction or are you going to instruct your students in the rationale?"

"Hmm. I hadn't thought about that," Lisa replied.

"I would highly encourage you to empower your students by sharing with them all of the research findings you will be using. Make these students active and equal partners in their education, and especially in understanding the strategies and related rationale that can help them do better at their job of learning. In my experience, I have found that empowering people to better themselves always results in their better performance."

"That makes perfect sense, Bill. I like being open with the students and actively involving them in many aspects of classroom management, so explaining why I am having them do what I ask them to do will be a natural fit."

"Excellent. Involve your students in as much of your classroom operation as you can, Lisa. That will give them a higher level of buy-in when they participate in the decision making. Solicit their ideas on how to make things work better—you'll be surprised at the good ideas they will offer. And be prepared to show your willingness to try their ideas if they sound reasonable. I guarantee that if you give them this kind of active role, it will contribute enormously to that trust relationship you told me was so important for learning. What you are talking about doing here is creating a highly successful learning team. So let them see and feel that they are important players. The payoffs will be huge.

"I also want to comment on the value-adding and waste elimination foci of your plan. Remember back a few weeks ago when I had asked you to list all of the activities you had done last year to teach your various units?

You had a list a mile long, and they were all good activities. Then after you decided you would make your units a week long, I asked you whether you could fit all of those activities in a week. I will never forget the look on your face as you looked at your list, then turned to me and gave me your answer of no. You mentally knew at that moment that you could not do all of those activities in your new plan, and it pained you to acknowledge that. Even though each of those activities added some value, you were able to use the decision matrix to prioritize and rate that value. Now that I see your end result and hear your rationale, I can see how your plan has incorporated only what adds value to the learning. When you only add value, you are, by definition, eliminating waste. Your students will only be getting the 'meat' of the curriculum from you, and you are asking them only to do what adds value to their learning. Neither you nor your students are doing wasteful busywork activities. I love how this plan respects the time and effort of both teacher and students. Respect for people is fundamental to lean, Lisa. Overall, from the lean perspective, this plan is customer-oriented and focuses on adding value. But it's also a genuine waste reduction effort with anticipated outcomes of increased performance from both teacher and students. Awesome job on this."

"Thank you, Bill."

"Now, I do have a few devil's advocate questions for you. Are you ready for them?"

"Sure, fire away."

Bill began his lean mentor questioning. "First question. Improvement is proven through measurement of the new way against the old way. Measurement data provide the proof. What is your plan for measuring improvement for you in delivering the curriculum and for the students in learning it? Your principal will undoubtedly ask you for the proof."

"Actually, he and I have already had a discussion on that very subject. The way I will be able to measure whether I teach the whole course is if I can complete instruction on every country of the world by the end of the school year. My plan as outlined in the planner should allow me to do that. The ultimate proof is actually pulling this off according to the plan I have developed on paper. Either I will teach everything or I won't. The planner has the documentation from week to week, and I will note any changes I must make each week in it so I can adjust my plan for next year, if need be."

Bill followed her rationale. "That will do for you, but what about for your students and their learning?"

"I have multiple measurements I am considering. For a macro view of the whole-class learning, I could compare the school performance score on the state standardized test in Geography at the end of the upcoming school year to the score from this past year. That should give a very clear picture of whether increased learning has happened in the whole class in this subject area," explained Lisa.

"How do you know that last year's score wasn't an anomaly?" asked Bill.

"I don't, but the scores ever since I've been here have been low."

"But you will want to prove with empirical data that your new approach has resulted in measurable learning improvement. One data point for comparison isn't adequate proof, Lisa, it just represents a possibility."

"So then maybe I should do the comparison with as many past scores as we have records for?"

"I think that would be a very good idea. And of course, scientifically, you will have to be able to repeat any improvement outcome at least three times using exactly the same method to prove your point."

"Okay, I can adjust that part of the measurement plan easily." Lisa opened her planner and wrote a quick note to record the change, then turned back to Bill. "Another way I was considering is comparing specific class section scores on various units to see whether the performance in different sections of this World Geography class shows the same performance trends. What do you think about that?"

Bill mulled that thought over. "I'm not sure that will provide the kind of proof you'd like. You have too many variables. A different set of kids from last year, as well as different organization and delivery of curriculum. Nope. I think for now you had better stick with the overall school performance scores. But beginning next year you can collect the trend data because you will have eliminated the curriculum variable."

"There's another measurement I'm planning on doing, but it's for another reason. Sometimes one unit can be more challenging than another. As a professional educator, I feel the need to determine whether my teaching is effective. If the kids in general had a particular problem in a unit, I really need to take a look at my delivery. It could be that I haven't made things clear enough. So I normally compare scores on weekly tests to help me pinpoint units that I may need to revamp for a better student learning outcome."

"That's a very good idea, Lisa. Since you brought up the notion of improvement ideas, I'd like to offer a very effective one that is easy to do. I don't think it will require any extra work on your part, but it could be extremely helpful in pinpointing opportunities for general teaching improvement on each unit, since I think that's what you are talking about, right?"

"Absolutely, Bill. What's your idea?"

"Have you ever heard of a thing called a Pareto analysis?" he asked.

Lisa shook her head. "No."

"A Pareto analysis categorizes occurrences by frequency. In the case of a test, you could use a Pareto to determine the top two questions that your students missed. Then you can focus improving your instruction in those two specific areas. Using that approach will help you reduce the variation in your student scores by resolving the two biggest problem areas that they have in each unit each time you teach it. Over time, you'll narrow your bell curve and skew it to the positive side of the midline. Does that make sense?"

Lisa visualized the curve Bill described and could see that if she routinely focused on remediating the top two problem areas for students, eventually that would result in a reduced spread of the bell curve limits, as well as the bell's positioning much closer to the higher scoring limit. "I get it, Bill. I already review how my lessons go over with the kids and make notes or actual changes immediately to my materials to capture the improvement for next year. And you're right. Since I already correct and analyze my tests for problem areas, I won't be doing anything extra. I'll just have a better focus for my improvement."

"Lisa, you are amazing. What I just heard you describe as your routine is continuous improvement, pure and simple. Like I said before, you have been a lean practitioner all along, you just didn't know it! And that's the beauty of lean—it really is plain common sense!" Bill's voice took on a more serious tone. "Now, you've got your plan to measure success on the macro level. Have you thought about how to measure success on a micro basis, at the individual student level?"

Lisa had thought about that and actually had several options for that measurement. "Students will have an individual score on the standardized Geography test that will tell whether or not they have achieved basic or proficient knowledge. We could use that performance as a measure of success. Another possibility would be the average of the unit tests or the individual report card grade in the class."

"It sounds like you have good options to discuss with your principal. It would be good to get his input on the final selection of those measures."

Lisa agreed.

"But I do have one other question for you," Bill added, "and that is in regard to the standardization of your and your students' weekly work routine, which, by the way, I really like. It's easy to comprehend and follow, and it strikes me as absolutely achievable, even in your short weeks. Part of your plan calls for the kids to take and use notes as study aids. I'm curious about that process. How do you have kids take notes, Lisa?"

"In the past I've just let them take notes on loose-leaf paper or in spiral notebooks, whatever their personal preference was."

"In the past? Does that mean you are contemplating a change for this year?"

Lisa admitted she wasn't sure what she was contemplating for this year beyond the kids taking notes. She described how students often had to be instructed in how to take notes and how to organize them to make the notes useful. Additionally, she wasn't sure those notes were optimized by the students as effective study tools. "Let me show you something, Bill." She went over to her filing cabinet, reached into the bottom drawer, and withdrew a file. She laid the file on the worktable, pulled a stapled packet from the file, and handed it to him. "This is a note packet that I use for another class I teach on ancient worlds. The kids use this same packet five times during the year, once for each of the five civilizations we study in the class. It's a special project assigned with each unit, but the kids also use it to study for tests. It's a whole lot easier to review five pages of notes than fifty-six pages in the textbook."

"So you have standardized your note packet for that class?"

"Yes, and as I was designing the standard work plan for the World Geography class, I wondered if I shouldn't somehow come up with a way to standardize the note-taking for it. I definitely do not want to do a packet. In the other class, I grade those note packets—they're assignments. In this class, neither the kids nor I will have time to do note packets each week."

Bill was intrigued. "Interesting. I was going to ask you about whether you had considered extending your standardization to your notes. Tell me, Lisa, why did you go to note packets in your other class?"

"There are several reasons, not the least of which is making things easier for the kids, and me, too."

Bill's eyebrows raised in surprise.

Seeing his reaction, Lisa offered an explanation. "I've told you that as a teacher I think it's important for my students to take notes. The process helps kids develop active listening and evaluative skills. But it also helps them learn organization."

"So you're using the packet to teach organization?"

Lisa nodded. "In the ancient worlds class, kids discover what makes a civilization a civilization. There are distinct components. To help the kids recognize and remember the components, I decided to create a note packet that is organized around those components. We use this same packet multiple times, once for each civilization. The same organization for each packet makes it easy for them to take notes and to find information. See," she flipped over the first page of the packet, "you'll always take and find notes you've taken on forms of transportation at the bottom of page two."

"So again you are using a pattern for learning."

Lisa laughed. "I guess so, but it wasn't intentional when I started. That's an unintended benefit. I wanted to find a way for me to easily assess and grade the students' note-taking as well as make it easy for the kids to organize their notes. You'll notice each of the categories and subcategories listed has a number in parentheses next to it?"

"Yes."

"That number represents the amount of points assigned to the requested information. That makes it easy for me to evaluate the score by section, and makes it equally easy for the kids to know how many points they are risking if they don't provide the called-for information. It's an assignment that actually doubles as a rubric."

"A what?" asked Bill.

"A rubric. It's like a score sheet. I use it to score the papers. The kids can use it in advance to check and make sure they have done a complete job—it helps them improve the quality of their performance."

"Lisa, there you go mistake-proofing again!" The words came out of Bill's mouth before he was even aware they were there.

"What?"

"You are creating a means to prevent mistakes or omissions from being made—that's mistake-proofing. No wonder you are doing so well with this project, you already have a mind-set tuned in to continuous improvement!" he congratulated her. "So what I hear you saying is that you're trying to figure out how to standardize your note taking in World Geography without having to deal with a note packet, is that it?"

"I'm trying to figure out what that would look like."

Bill flipped through the pages of the note packet. "You said the kids spend some time filling these out?"

"Yes," Lisa replied. "They have about six weeks for each unit in that class." A look of revelation spread across Lisa's face. "Omigosh!" She quickly grabbed a blank piece of paper and listed a dozen words down the left side of the page, then turned the paper so Bill could view her writing. "We don't have time for a packet. We just need a note sheet each week. I can standardize the sheets and create the pattern for the note taking and review by simply making a one-page template that lists the categories of information we will always discuss in each unit. If I run them off and provide them for the students to fill in each week, that would be standardizing that learning tool, right?" (See Figure 5.)

Bill smiled at Lisa's excitement. "Absolutely! And that idea seems to be supported by your learning theory. I'll tell you what, Lisa, I'd better give you a few last words and get out of your way because it seems to me that you don't need me anymore."

Name

Country =											
Category											
Longitude/latitude											
Climate											
Capitol city											
Geography											
Natural resources											
High tech?											
Trade products/partners											
Money unit											
Official language(s)											
Identifying arts/music											
Social classes?											
Education for all?											
Role of men											
Role of women											
Sense of family											
Organized religion											
Cultural traditions											

Figure 5 Notesheet example.

WINNING APPROVAL

Seated at the conference table in her principal's office, Lisa reached into her school bag and retrieved two folders, one of which she handed to Todd, who sat next to her; the other she opened on the table before her.

"Thank you for making time to review this with me today, Todd. If we decide something needs to be changed, I wanted the three weeks before school starts to make those adjustments."

"No problem, Lisa. In fact, you and this project have been on my mind all summer. I appreciate the e-mail updates you've sent, but I'm anxious to learn about all the details and see your finished product."

"Not as anxious as I am to show you!" Lisa responded. "I'll tell you, Todd, I really feel that going through this experience has enlightened me on how to become a better teacher. I've had to seriously analyze and evaluate what is essential for learning to happen in my classroom. And that's given me a high level of confidence that what I'm proposing to do is absolutely going to result in advanced learning."

The conviction in Lisa's voice captured Todd's full attention. "I'm all for that. Fill me in," he invited.

Lisa began her briefing by introducing the general concepts of lean and load leveling and how she had adapted them to the process of curriculum delivery. She reviewed the rationale for the project—to ensure that the entire assigned curriculum was delivered in such a way that the students would master it. "When we talked last spring, you recognized the potential long-term benefit if this program works and is adopted throughout the school. The failure to deliver assigned curriculum year-to-year throughout a student's thirteen-year school career compounds learning gaps, even for students who do well. The kids don't get the opportunity to learn everything they could, and teachers lose the opportunity to teach everything they are assigned when they have to spend time shoring up learning that didn't take place in the year or years before. It's a huge waste for both students and teachers. If every teacher was able to complete their curriculum delivery in a way that promotes students mastering it, that problem wouldn't exist, and learning levels would increase."

Guiding Todd through the syllabus she had developed for World Geography (see Figures 6 and 7), Lisa explained how her plan was predicated on finishing the study of world nations—all of them—by year's end. She described how she had created week-long units to both amortize and accomplish her task, and she shared her weekly standard work and the rationale behind every teaching and learning decision she had made. Fascinated by Lisa's inclusive planning and the logic behind it, Todd listened attentively. "Are you sure you can teach everything you have scheduled for each week in a week's time?" he asked.

"I've given that particular attention, and my answer is yes. But there is a caveat to that statement, which is in *your* hands." Lisa then pointed out the two catch-up weeks she had built into her schedule as a hedge against unforeseen interruptions. "The caveat is, if the interruptions exceed my ability to work around them with these two weeks, I won't be able to finish the curriculum. I'm relying on *you* to protect my instructional time, Todd. If you do, the work routine I've planned will allow me to teach everything I've assigned to a specific week, regardless of whether there are three or four or five teaching days in that week. Each week's unit is specifically planned for the number of teaching days on the calendar for that week."

Todd committed his intention to protect her instructional time as best he could, assuring Lisa that he wanted her plan to work. "I am concerned, though, about your testing frequency. Weekly testing is a lot to ask of kids, don't you think? And it eliminates an entire class period each week that could be used for instruction."

Lisa explained how she had asked herself those same questions and, after much soul-searching and a brief discussion with Bill just to have a different perspective, she felt that weekly tests were actually beneficial. "In the past, Todd, I have done end-of-continent tests, midterms, and a final exam that covered the whole year. The results were terrible. Do you know why? I firmly believe it was because there was too much material covered on each assessment, which made it nearly impossible for kids to prepare for them. Plus, students are procrastinators. Long periods of time between assessments aren't good for them, and it certainly doesn't help me as a teacher to immediately catch and remediate a problem when a student encounters one. A weekly exam provides an incentive for kids to keep up, it limits the

Week of	Country(s) to be covered	Pages in the text	Quiz date	Notes
Sept 8–11	First week of school—rules of operation, review, project			Assign special project
Sept 14–18	Map skills, geography themes, geography patterns			
Sept 21–25	Complete global pattern maps, pretest, begin United States review			
Sept 28–Oct 2	United States and Canada	89–131	Oct 2	
Oct 5–9	Mexico, Central America, and the West Indies	153–183	Oct 9	
Oct 12–16	West Indies	183–193	Oct 16	
Oct 19–23	Brazil and its neighbors	195–210	Oct 23	
Oct 26–30	Andes countries	217–232	Oct 30	
Nov 2–6	British Isles and Scandinavia	255–270	Nov 7	
Nov 9–13	France, Germany, Benelux, and Alpine countries	277–293	Nov 13	
Nov 16–20	Portugal, Spain, Italy and Greece	297–313	Nov 20	
Nov 23–27	Czech Republic, Slovakia, the Balkans	332–338	Nov 25	Short week—Thanksgiving
Nov 30–Dec 4	Baltic republics, Poland, Hungary	319–331	Dec 4	
Dec 7–11	Russia and independent lands	348–376	Dec 11	
Dec 14–18	Student presentations on special project/Catch-up		No quiz	
Dec 21–Jan 1	Christmas break			No school
Jan 4–8	Independent, Caucasus, Central Asia republics	383–399	Jan 8	
Jan 11–15	SW Asia, Turkey, Lebanon, Syria, Jordan	408–430	Jan 15	
Jan 18–22	Arabian peninsula, Iran, Iraq, Afghanistan	431–438	Jan 22	
Jan 25–29	Israel	423–427	Jan 29	

Continued

Figure 6   World Geography course syllabus.

Week of	Country(s) to be covered	Pages in the text	Quiz date	Notes
Feb 1–5	*Exodus*—the film / Catch-up		No quiz	
Feb 8–12	Middle East discussions		No quiz	Opinion paper due
Feb 15–19	North Africa, the Sahel countries	444–461; 470–473; 490–493	Feb 19	
Feb 22–26	Nigeria and the coastal countries	484–489; 494–501	Feb 26	
Mar 1–5	East Africa	521–538	Mar 5	
Mar 8–12	Central Africa	505–517	Mar 12	
Mar 15–19	Spring break			No school
Mar 22–26	Environmental camp		No quiz	No classes all week
Mar 29–Apr 2	Antarctica	718–723	Mar 31	Short week—Easter
Apr 5–9	South Africa	545–564	Apr 9	
Apr 12–16	South Asia and subcontinent	574–598	Apr 16	
Apr 19–23	Himalayan and island countries	599–602	Apr 23	
Apr 26–30	China	609–626	Apr 30	
May 3–7	Japan and the Koreas	633–648	May 7	
May 10–14	Mainland SE Asia, 7 Islands	655–668	May 14	
May 17–21	New Zealand and Oceania	678–692	May 21	
May 24–28	Australia	703–723	May 26	Short week
May 31–Jun 4	Wrap-up week—Geography Bee, World competition Celebrate doing the entire curriculum!!!		No quiz	Report cards done

Figure 6 *Continued*

World Geography—Standard Weekly Learning Routine

The following schedule of World Geography study will be followed. This syllabus is provided to students as a planning tool. At a glance, you know what to expect and when to expect it each week during the school year.

From time to time, students may involve themselves in activities that provide the option of missing one or more classes. While it is your choice to miss class, your responsibility for your schoolwork is not subject to that option: you will be responsible for finding out what you missed, learning the material, and meeting deadlines, including the taking of exams. Please bear that in mind as you make your choices.

For the most part, each week will be structured as follows:

- *Monday*—Lecture on physical features, natural resources, government, economy of the country(s) for the week.
  - Give out five international news articles, which will be on Friday's quiz.
  - Give out dilemma for discussion on Thursday.
  - Give out topographical map form and instruction sheet.
  - Post Carmen Sandiego clue for the week on famous person/place/thing from the country(s) of the week.
- *Tuesday*—Lecture on history, language, religion, cultural highlights.
  - Post second Carmen Sandiego clue for the week.
- *Wednesday*—Class time provided for completion of map work; bring colored pencils.
  - Post third Carmen Sandiego clue for the week; listen to music from the area. Possibly sample food/craft, game from area studied.
- *Thursday*—Discussion of a dilemma pertinent to the country(s)/area.
  - Post fourth Carmen Sandiego clue for the week.
- *Friday* – Quiz, turn in map.
  - Post Carmen Sandiego results.
  - Special project checkpoint.
  - Students may begin pre-reading the next week's section after they have turned in their quiz.

Carmen Sandiego Competition: Each week, Carmen Sandiego will kidnap or steal a famous person, place, or thing from the area studied. Four clues will be posted over the week to help students determine the identity of the missing person, place, or thing. These items will not be covered in class lectures and will require personal research on the student's own time. Only one guess per student will be accepted in the weekly competition. Answers will be submitted in writing on Fridays at the beginning of class. The answer will be announced during class on Friday. Tally for each student will be kept and posted throughout the year. During the last week of the term, the grade winner will be determined by the highest overall score. Should a tie exist, a geography face-off will determine the winner. The prize is _____.

Exams and Special Projects: Exams will be limited to weekly quizzes. One special project—the International Study Project—will be assigned during the first trimester. One special project—Video Bingo—will be assigned during the second and third trimesters.

Geography Bee: Students will participate in a year-end geography competition to test overall knowledge of world geography. Not graded.

Figure 7   Standard weekly learning routine.

amount of material they have to master, thereby making it more doable, and it will enable me to be a more responsive teacher. If there's a problem this week, I can identify and intervene immediately, not discover it weeks down the line when the wrong learning is already cemented. A weekly test will also serve as a quality check for the students," she stated, repeating Bill's argument. "They'll know from week to week how they are performing, and that will give them the opportunity to take improvement actions before it's too late. The other advantage I see is that the grade I will compile using weekly exams will be a much more accurate reflection of performance than one that is made up of only one or two exam scores over a term."

"Yes, I can see those advantages," Todd agreed.

"There's also another advantage that supports advanced learning in the weekly exam structure I'm envisioning. I'm planning to give 100-question tests, and the questions will be cumulative."

"Cumulative?"

"Yes. I'm not going to give my students permission to forget what we've already learned. That would be a terrible waste. I'm planning to forewarn the kids that any material we've already covered is fair game on tests. While the vast majority of the 100 questions I ask will be from that week's unit, I plan to recycle ten or more questions each week. This does three things: First, the students will have to continually review. Secondly, it will allow me to retest on a topic that may not have been clearly understood the first time around—I have a means of tracking the most-missed questions for that purpose. The third benefit is tied to learning theory. When students have to think about a test question and formulate the correct answer, by that very act they are reteaching themselves that concept. So to address your concern about losing a day of instruction to give a test, I actually feel that the test is a reinforcement to the learning, and therefore a continuation of the week's instruction. In fact, that instruction will continue yet again when I give back the test and go over the test questions. The test follow-up will provide another opportunity for the students to self-reteach. It's part of my plan for mastery learning."

Todd's concentration on Lisa's arguments was evident as he leaned forward in his chair. "Tell me more about how this plan will promote mastery learning, especially if you are only spending a week teaching each unit. Do you really think it's possible for students to master all the information in such a short period of time? What you're proposing is a really rigorous learning plan, Lisa."

Lisa had anticipated his concern and was eager to share her strategy. Calling his attention to the syllabus and standard work documents, Lisa described for Todd how she had incorporated both brain and learning research into the development of her standard work. She would be providing the opportunity for ten impressions of the information to be made in different formats for the students over a number of days. "The research shows that ten impressions is the number needed for information to be stored in long-term memory for recall. The activities I have selected for our classroom time, as well as the homework assignments I plan to give, which you can see are minimal, will provide those ten impressions if the kids do them."

"That's a big if," commented Todd.

"That's true," agreed Lisa, "but I plan to tell the kids right away *why* I am doing what I am doing and why I am asking them to do the few assignments I give. My intent is to put them into a more active role in their learning. My mentor, Bill, calls it empowerment, and that's really what it is—empowering kids to *know how* to do a good job. I will be giving those students who really have the desire to do well the means to do just that. Will they respond the way I want them to? Let me ask you this, Todd: if I gave you a surefire way to improve your performance that was pretty simple to pull off and it ended up working, wouldn't you do it?"

"Have you thought about parent reaction to this rigor?" Todd asked.

Lisa took a moment to form her response to the potential concern of parents. "I believe most parents want the best education experience possible for their children. I don't know that reasonable rigor will upset them, but a significant and unanticipated surprise definitely will. My plan for parents is similar to my plan for students. I'm going to tell them up front and clearly what I am going to do and why I have chosen to do it. I plan to give each student as well as each parent or guardian a copy of the year's syllabus and the standard weekly work routine, and discuss it thoroughly. I'll do that in class during the first week of school with the students, and I will do that at open house night with the parents. My personal belief is that when parents understand how doable it is and that it won't require extra work on their part, they will support it because it will result in better learning for their children."

Todd sat back in his chair. What she had said, all of it, made a lot of sense.

Pulling out the note sheet she had developed, Lisa pointed out that when students repeatedly used it as a learning tool each week, they would become very familiar with the organization of the material. That, she believed, would allow for quicker review and study, and contribute to the advancement of their learning. "The long and the short of it, Todd," she concluded, "is that doing this in the way I have planned precisely follows the research recipe for successful long-term learning. It will allow me to teach the entire curriculum I've been assigned to deliver this year. That will reduce the waste of time involved in someone else having to finish teaching it later. It will allow me to be more responsive in interventions. It will provide a greater opportunity for kids to be able to learn the material. And, yes, I have set a rigorous schedule to meet an aggressive goal. But I really believe that this plan will allow me, as well as the kids, to achieve it."

Lisa awaited her principal's reaction. He sat in thoughtful contemplation, his fingers laced on the tabletop before him. Finally, a smile crept across Todd's face as he shook his head in wonderment. "A few months ago in this very office I told you I admired the educational leadership your willingness to take on this new project demonstrated. After hearing you explain this extremely well-thought-out plan, seeing the detail with which you have analyzed and put together the teaching schedule, and the research basis of your curriculum design, I am even more impressed. Clearly, we don't know for sure whether this will result in advanced learning, but if ever there was a well-designed experiment that was worthy of a test, Lisa, this is it. You have my okay on it." Todd extended his hand and Lisa shook it eagerly.

"Thank you," she said simply, "I appreciate your support."

"Now," Todd continued as he leaned back in his chair and assumed a more relaxed posture, "let's assume that things will work as you project. We need to plan a measurement system that will accurately measure success or failure in a way that will be indisputable, totally black and white." Lisa shared with Todd the ideas she had discussed with Bill. After some deliberation, they agreed that completing the curriculum as laid out in her planner would conclusively demonstrate its total delivery. They also decided that comparison of the school performance score on the standardized state achievement test in geography at the end of the year with the school's performance average on previous years' tests would be an acceptable initial "proof" of advanced learning. Todd agreed with Bill's recommendation that real proof would require a three-year trend of improved scores. "If the results of this year's score are what you expect, we will automatically plan on extending this experiment for a minimum of two more years."

For measuring at the micro level, which Todd also supported, he recommended Lisa use a multiple measurement system to provide assessment from several different perspectives. She would use the individual student scores on the year-end standardized geography test as one measure of success and the student's report card grade as another. He also asked her to chart test scores for all sections of her class and compare means and trends of those different student populations. But Todd also asked Lisa to compare overall report card scores from the past years she had taught the class with the report card scores for this year. "I know your curriculum is going to be different this year, and that will put a variable in the mix, but we may get some insight on whether improvement in learning is indicated from looking at that data. By itself, it isn't anything. But taken in context with the rest of the measurements, it might lend additional insight. It's worth taking a look at it." Lisa left Todd's office feeling that her idea and efforts were

THE FIRST DAY OF SCHOOL

Like all teachers who have taught in a school for more than a year, Lisa had developed a reputation among students. Kids talk about their experiences in classrooms. Brothers and sisters who have formerly had a teacher contribute to the expectations of their younger siblings who subsequently are assigned to that same educator. Lisa's reputation was one of a good teacher who had high academic expectations, who truly cared about her students as individual people, and who liked to make learning fun.

With that reputation as their guide, students made their way into Lisa's classroom with the synergy that comes from meeting up with old friends for a new adventure. Having stationed herself in the hall just outside the classroom doorway, Lisa personally greeted each arriving student, as well as those former students who passed by on their way to a different destination. Laughter, energy, and milling bodies filled every school space as the sound of the bell blared the official start of the first class period.

"Good morning everyone," Lisa announced as she closed the classroom door behind her and moved to the front of the room. "Welcome to your homeroom and first period—World Geography! For those of you who don't know me, my name is Ms. Randolph. I am very happy to have each and every one of you as my student. Your teachers from last year have told me to expect great things from this class, and I am very excited about that because that means we will be able to do some incredible things together! Now, I want to hear a lot about you, and I want to tell you a little about myself, but first we need to get settled and take care of some essentials. So please take a desk wherever you want for right now." The familiar sounds of shuffling feet, textbooks thudding on desktops, and the low murmur of excited whispers as students found a place to sit brought a smile to Lisa's face. In her mind, there could never be a more exciting sound than the musical rhapsody of the first day of school.

After her students had settled in, Lisa called their attention to several questions she had written out on the whiteboard at the front of the class. "While I am taking attendance and lunch count and collecting all of your beginning-of-the-year paperwork," she instructed them, "I want you to be giving some thought to these questions so you will have answers ready when we do introductions in just a few moments." Lisa took care of her housekeeping chores and then turned back to the class. She asked for a student volunteer to begin the get-acquainted activity, one that involved revealing some trivial personal information as directed on the board, something cool the student had done over the summer, and an anticipated expectation for the World Geography class. "And I want your honest opinion, even if it's negative."

The first volunteer provided the answers to the introductory questions, recounted the summer spent hanging out with friends, then offered the first opinion of the class. "Everybody says you're a great teacher, Ms. Randolph, but I mean, how exciting can geography be? No offense."

Lisa laughed along with her students. "None taken, Jake. When I took geography for the first time, I found it to be awfully boring myself!" Lisa's comment raised eyebrows and elicited some surprised guffaws. "You'll be relieved to know," she continued, "that I've worked pretty hard at making your World Geography class not boring for either you or me!"

Lisa's candid remarks facilitated a comfortable continuation of the round-robin introductions. Having heard even negative opinions respected, students easily shared information and stories as well as their predispositions to the World Geography class. Lisa listened carefully, picking up a significant level of negative anticipation and anxiety from the students about taking a class they perceived was going to be hard because of its scope. She decided she would wait until the next day to address that concern, and concentrate on building enthusiasm and rapport that first day.

The students enjoyed the opportunity to reacquaint themselves and catch up on what everyone had been doing. When it was her turn to talk about herself, Lisa shared some off-the-wall personal facts that she knew the kids would enjoy hearing. "You see," she pointed out, "There's a bizarre side to me, too!" Then she told the students about her summer. "Unlike all of you, I didn't spend my summer on vacation or at the pool or visiting places of interest. What I did do was sort of go to school and do homework all summer here in this classroom."

Several students gasped. Looks of shock registered on their faces as the class responded with a cacophony of "What?" "That's sick!" "You've got to be kidding!" and similar expressions of disbelief. "That's no vacation!" Jake insisted.

It was Lisa's turn to chuckle. "Actually, I enjoyed what I did this summer a lot because I completely made over the World Geography class you will be taking, and I am really excited about all the things you are going to get to do, like eat new foods from around the world. Anybody in here like to eat?" Every hand in the class shot up. "Yes, well, we'll be doing some feasting from time to time. Who likes music?" Another set of hands were enthusiastically launched skyward. "Great! Because we're also going to listen to music from around the world and perhaps try learning a dance or two. You're going to examine neat things you've never seen, like witch doctor bones from Africa and a water current and star map made out of coconut husks and seashells that people from the Polynesian islands in the Pacific Ocean use to guide their canoes between the different islands. You're going to learn about different customs so when you meet people from foreign countries you'll know how to greet them properly and not accidentally insult them. There's just a ton of neat things about this world of ours that you're going to discover in this class. And I had a great time this summer putting this all together for you."

For the rest of the period, Lisa guided her students through an activity that defined the way their class would operate for the entire year. "Think about this: you will probably spend more time here at school each day than you will at your own house. I know I will. So it makes sense for us to set up this classroom and the way it works to be comfortable for all of us, and that's what we're going to do right now—establish how we're going to operate and treat each other as a school family. This isn't my classroom—it's *our* second home. So today *we're* going to collaborate on how to make this a safe and fair place to get our work done." While Lisa had routinely used this activity to set the stage for cooperation, she now saw an added importance in its contribution to laying a foundation for empowerment and the trust partnership she and Bill had agreed would be critical to making her plan succeed. By the end of the period, she and the students had fashioned a code of operation and behavior that everyone agreed to abide by. Lisa was pleased with the respect-based constitution her students had developed. Unbeknownst to them, they had participated in laying another block in the foundation of her lean load-leveling plan.

Lisa repeated this process with the other five classes she taught. Students in her World Geography and other Social Studies classes received their first homework assignment of putting a protective cover on their textbook. "And I want you to page through the entire book to see what all we're going to cover this year. We'll talk about that first thing tomorrow."

The first day was, as first days always are, a great day.

"How'd today go?" asked Bill when he and Lisa talked by phone later that evening. He listened attentively as Lisa recounted the introductory activities she had conducted in each class throughout the day, as well as the information those activities had revealed.

"I think today was very successful in setting the stage for student ownership and empowerment, Bill. The kids were eager to state their voice and know it was both heard and applied to our rules of operation. Each year when I do this, I see an immediate change in attitude, even from potential problem kids. Starting off by making them equal partners with me in how we treat each other and deal with issues really settles things down in a hurry. Having this accomplished today will allow us to address content tomorrow."

Bill congratulated Lisa on her first day's strategy. "Your decision to survey for their expectations for the class was an excellent approach—it's good to know the gremlins up front. And the collaboration on the operating rules is essential for establishing trust. It sounds like they already feel a level of empowerment just from today. You did a nice job, Lisa. So what is your plan for tomorrow?"

Lisa outlined her intended introduction of lean methods and load leveling to optimize the students' personal learning. "I think the best approach is from the customer point of view, Bill. They need to see that what I am going to ask them to do will actually be easier for them than the old way. I anticipate they will be as apprehensive as I was when I was trying to figure out how to accomplish the whole course in thirty-two weeks. I need to help them believe it's doable. The impact on their mastery learning will be a secondary thing for them right now. But I have an idea on how to deal with that."

"Good. I agree with you about approaching this from the student perspective. But before you tell them how it will make their work easier, consider giving them a purpose for working at all. People will work if they have a purpose—what we're going to do, why we're going to do it, how we're going to do it. Also, be sure you give the kids the big-picture view, the systemic view of the plan. Remember how enlightening it was for you to understand how everything fit and worked together."

Bill's recommendations spurred further reflection in Lisa. Having purpose—she could envision how she would address that with her students the next day.

"Thanks for that advice; it all makes sense. Tomorrow I'm going to be brutally honest—it's my style, and, frankly, I think the kids prefer it that way. They don't like surprises any more than I do. So laying it all out and addressing their concerns up front is the tack I'm going to take."

"Sounds good," Bill concluded. "You really have done a superb job with your planning, Lisa. But even superb plans can encounter unforeseen challenges. Expect challenges to come up because they will. My advice to you is, when one arises, first use your common sense to resolve it. But if the solution isn't clear or evades you, bring the kids fully into the problem-solving process. That's where the empowerment you've begun really pays off. Good luck. Keep me posted, and call me if you need to talk things out."

As she settled down to go to sleep later that evening, Lisa envisioned how she would carry out day two of her plan. Tomorrow, she realized, was really the day she had been preparing for all summer.

INTRODUCING LEAN AND THE LOAD LEVELING PLAN TO STUDENTS

Spirits were still high as students entered Lisa's World Geography class the next day. Asked for comments on the textbook they had previewed the night before, the kids offered a number of remarks, including one by the previous day's jokester.

"This book covers a lot of countries, Ms. R," piped up Jake. "Are you sure we need to cover all of them? I've never even heard of some of them." Jake's suggestion for a negotiated reduction in work before work even started amused Lisa—it was a typical middle school student tactic. The bizarre nature of the suggestion prompted some snickers of laughter.

"And that's precisely why we need to learn about all of them, Jake," Lisa retorted with a twinkle in her eye, "because I know you're the kind of guy who wants and needs to know everything!"

The whole class laughed.

Lisa waited for the chuckling to die down. "Seriously, Jake's question is a valid one. Why do we need to cover the whole book? Well, there are two reasons. The first involves me. I've been hired to teach you this course. It's my responsibility to teach you about the whole world, not just a part of it. If your Mom or Dad failed to carry out his or her job responsibility, what would you expect the consequences for them might be?" She paused for the students to contemplate what she had suggested and waited for a response.

"They could get fired or something?" one student asked.

"People can, indeed, lose their jobs if they do not fulfill their job requirements. That's true throughout the world of work. So I hope you can see why it is important from my standpoint to fulfill my job responsibility to teach you everything in this book."

The students had Lisa's full attention and nodded their understanding. Their teacher continued.

"The second reason we need to cover the whole book doesn't involve me. It involves you. Right now you might be thinking, 'knowing geography isn't important in my life.' But in a couple of years, all of you will be getting a job. You will be working with people from various cultures, just as you are sitting among students from various cultures today. Understanding a person's culture is a key to understanding how to work and get along with them, and that understanding can help you get and keep a job. A job is necessary so you can earn money to buy the things you want. Many companies today have customers who are located all around the world. It then becomes essential to know where your customers are and how to deal with them, which again requires an understanding of their culture. So as unimportant as geography might seem right now in your life, before long it will be a very important understanding for you to have, and I want to help you get it. You and I each have a World Geography mission. Mine is to teach it; yours is to learn it. That, in a nutshell, is the purpose for us being here and doing what we're doing.

"Now, there are a couple of ways we can accomplish our mission. One way is to establish a classroom of students, and the other way is to establish a learning team. In a classroom of students, the teacher is the center of the learning, is the one making all the decisions, and keeps everyone focused on their work. In a learning team, the students and teacher collaborate as equal partners, they learn from each other as co-teachers and are co-decision-makers in solving classroom problems. In a learning team environment, students take responsibility for keeping themselves focused on their work. Which environment sounds more appealing to you?"

A quick discussion ensued in which students offered additional attributes of each learning environment type. Subsequent to that discussion, the kids voiced unanimous preference for the learning team approach. Knowing the innate desires of middle schoolers, Lisa had been confident they would choose the option that gave them an active voice and role in the management of the classroom. What had Bill said? Empowerment engages?

"Well, I agree with you," she complimented her students. "I much prefer the learning team approach myself. It allows me to treat you like adults. I think you're ready for it, and I suspect you'd prefer that, wouldn't you?"

Heads around the classroom nodded in concurrence.

Lisa continued. "But, more importantly, learning teams can accomplish more than individual students can. When we work at learning together, we can figure out how to learn much more and do it better than if we tried to learn by ourselves. We support and help each other just like players on a sports team."

"Team World Geography?" queried Jake impishly.

Lisa chuckled. "Yes, Team World Geography, Jake. And I am your learning coach! Let me tell you how I envision this working."

For the rest of the class period Lisa outlined her load leveling plan. She handed out a copy of the class syllabus to every student and went over the details of the calendar. She explained how each week's grouping had been based on the connectedness the countries have with one another as well as the amount of time needed to teach the material. The students, in turn, asked the question Lisa anticipated they would: how could they possibly learn it all?

"Excellent question. Let me tell you about my plan for your success."

Lisa passed out the standard work sheets she had prepared that listed the weekly routine her class would follow. She reminded the students that everyone learns in patterns, and identified the pattern of learning they would follow each week. Then Lisa displayed the standard note sheet she had developed on the board. She explained how it would be an important tool for them in developing important active listening and decision-making skills. Using it would also make their studying easier by helping them organize their learning in a similar pattern each week.

"I respect you too much to waste your time, so I won't give you any busywork in this class. That's a promise. Everything I am going to ask you to do I feel is absolutely necessary for you to do to learn the material. If it's not essential, I won't ask you to do it. Let's take a look at what you will have for homework," she proposed.

Lisa was careful to point out that, as listed on the standard work sheet, routine weekly homework would consist of reading over the notes taken in class, drawing the topographical map, reading a couple of newspaper articles she would provide, and talking to friends and family about a dilemma question that they would then discuss in class on Thursday. By doing each classroom and homework activity, she explained, students would accomplish precisely what brain and learning research said was necessary for them to master their learning—get ten impressions of the material.

"This whole plan is designed for your success and all of it is based on proven research. Oh yes, and there's one final plus I'm sure you'll like," she offered. "With a weekly test you won't have to study great quantities of information to study for tests, only one week's information at a time."

"Well," piped in Jake, "what about chapter exams?"

"No chapter exams, no midterm exams, and no final exams in this plan," Lisa said emphatically.

For a split second, as the full impact of her words registered, the class was quiet and then thunderous cheering and clapping erupted. "Yeah!" they all shouted, pounding desktops in approval.

Lisa smiled in appreciation of their delight. She had hooked them, at least for the time being.

"Since I'm being honest with you about everything, I have to tell you that there is one catch. You know as well as I do that if you don't practice something you'll forget how to do it, right?" The students nodded their understanding. "As your coach, I can't let you forget your learning. So what we will do to keep your learning active is, on each week's test I'll include a few review questions from units we've already studied. It's like practicing a sports move you've already learned—you know it, but your coach asks you to do it again to keep it fresh. It's the same principle. Once you've already gotten information into your long-term memory, it's just practicing what you already know and keeping it fresh."

For the most part, the students were persuaded by the logic of Lisa's plan as well as by her confidence in it. They were willing to give it a chance, especially when their teacher assured them they would be active participants in resolving any unanticipated problems if they arose.

"Okay, then. You each have a copy of the syllabus, our standard routine, and the note sheet. Those copies are for you. I'm going to give another copy to your parents next week at the grade-level open house so they will understand how we are going to operate as a learning team and how we will carry out our learning plan. But I want you to share with them tonight everything that we talked about today. Get them started in their understanding. As a team we're going to be all about open and frequent communication. Come with questions tomorrow if you think of more because I want to get them all answered."

Throughout the rest of the day during her World Geography classes, Lisa carried out a version of her first rollout. She was able to refine it each time by incorporating and addressing the concerns voiced by the students in the previous classes. She was gratified that the students had received her pitch with a willingness to try the plan, although some expressed some reservations and skepticism that they could learn enough of the week's material to pass a test each Friday. *That,* she told herself, *is my next challenge. I have to orchestrate a first success to cement their belief that it will work.*

SETTLING IN

Over the next week, Lisa introduced her students to the lean organization of her classroom. She explained her own discovery and how it had made her work easier, and assured them that keeping up that organization would do the same for them.

Students did preliminary activities designed to point out the patterns in learning geography. They saw how understanding where the basic wind currents and water currents were allowed them to predict climate, and how various land features could do the same. Viewing the rings of fire around the world surprised the kids, who beforehand had no idea volcanoes were connected to tectonic plate edges. Coloring a world climate map revealed a relationship of climate zones to latitude. A similar relationship became obvious comparing population and climate zone maps. Students began to see the cause-and-effect relationships inherent in geography. Slowly but surely, Lisa stripped away the layers of mystery and difficulty from the study of geography by building a general understanding of the subject based on recognizing and learning from patterns.

After laying the groundwork of doability, Lisa next introduced the special project her students would have over the first term, the International Study Project. This assignment called for each student to study in detail a country from their personal ethnic background. While hoping to help students come to a deeper appreciation of their family roots and background, Lisa also used the assignment to teach students project management skills. It was a big assignment with 24 components. All students balked at it when it was initially given out, which is precisely what their teacher expected. Over the years, Lisa had found that students groused not at the assignment itself, but because they didn't know how to organize and chunk a large project into manageable bites. She explained how they would be able to accomplish this task using the weekly checkpoints.

"We will, as a learning community, be supporting each other throughout this entire project. So each Friday we'll have a checkpoint to keep us on track. You'll be choosing what components you want to work on each week to meet the deadline. I won't let anyone fall through the cracks. Remember, I'll be coaching you through it." She explained that over the years her students had confided that the most important thing they got out of doing the International Study Project was the realization that they could handle anything. "That's an understanding and confidence I want all of you to have, too, and that's why I'm asking you to do it."

The Carmen Sandiego game was presented as an intellectual challenge, with a prize drawing from among those who identified the most correct answers over the term. Competition is the lifeblood of most middle schoolers, and with Lisa's daily clues and the fun format she established for securing answers on Friday, everyone enjoyed participating, although not all students were serious in researching the clues. Lisa was satisfied to motivate those interested in enhanced learning, knowing that the others would gain additional learning just by being part of the activity.

By Friday of the first week, students had gotten a taste of what operating as a learning team in World Geography class would be like, and their enthusiasm level was still high. By the end of the second week, Lisa had introduced the new program to parents at the grade-level open house night. Most of them had already heard about the learning team and load leveling concepts from their children. They had had a chance to pre-think their concerns as well as observe their children's reaction to two weeks of the approach. Lisa's detailed explanation of the research basis of her plan satisfied most parent concerns. She went through the syllabus, laying out the week-by-week plan that would allow students to complete the study of the entire world. She described their standard work routine, which would include discussion with parents and friends of a weekly dilemma, a means of keeping the parents abreast of and involved in the learning activities of their children. She assured the parents that the program did not require parent responsibility beyond open communication with her and supporting students in completing the minimal homework assignments given.

"It's essential that they have the ten impressions of the material in order to master it. Reviewing their notes each night as homework will provide almost half of those ten impressions," Lisa said in conclusion. "That should only take fifteen minutes per night. If you set the expectation that your child will spend that amount of time each night reviewing those notes and working on the map, and hold him or her to that expectation, I guarantee your student will be successful."

On Friday of week three, Lisa spent part of her class time previewing the full kick-in of the syllabus on the next Monday. She wanted to review the weekly plan and get things fresh in the minds of students so precious class time would not be needed for that review in what would now be very tight weekly schedules.

"I want to congratulate you all—you've done a great job these past three weeks. The things we've worked on have given you a general background of knowledge that will be helpful as you begin studying the world in earnest next week." Lisa displayed the course syllabus on the wall and called the students' attention to the first week's unit of study. "On Monday, we're going to start here in the U.S. where we live. I know you've already studied a little of our country's geography back in fifth grade as part of your U.S. History class, so this won't be completely new to you. We will also be covering Canada. You can see that next week is the first of thirty-two units that will take us completely around the world, one section at a time."

Lisa changed the wall display to reveal the standard work routine. "So, here's the plan for next week. As you can see, when you get in Monday, you're going to be receiving some materials from me at the beginning of class. You'll get a dilemma question that I want you to talk about with everybody here at school and at home, and hear what they have to say on the subject. I know talking is right up your alley." The students chuckled in agreement. "We'll be discussing what you think is the answer and your justification next Thursday. Also on Monday you'll be getting a sheet with a couple of newspaper articles about world events that I will choose from the Sunday newspaper. All I want you to do is read them. You need to become aware of what is going on in different places in the world. I will ask a general question about at least one of them on the test next Friday, but if you have read the article, you'll be able to answer it. You'll also get a blank outline map of Canada and the U.S. and an instruction sheet so you can make it look like the map in your book. You'll have all week to do that. And finally, you'll get a blank note sheet. On Monday, you'll be starting to take notes in class. I recommend you read the pages in the text this weekend, but frankly, I know many of you won't. We don't have time to read the text in class, so I will be giving you all the important information I want you to learn during class. You're going to take notes on what you hear and see, and then you're going to read over those notes as homework. Remember at the beginning of the year when I explained how your brains work and what it takes to learn? Can anyone tell me how many times you have to think about something before you can remember it?"

A hand shot up. "Ten."

Lisa nodded. "That's right, you have to seriously think about something ten times to remember it. Remember, I also told you that what I ask you to do each day is part of a weekly plan to make sure you have ten opportunities to think about the material. Those ten opportunities include your classwork and your homework. If you do everything I ask you to do, you'll have the ten you need. If you choose not to do what I ask, you won't have the ten impressions research says is required for learning. So take a look at this plan one more time before we start it. We'll review it again briefly on Monday. But be ready to get started first thing. Have a good weekend!"

Before she knew it, the weekend had passed, and Lisa was handing out note sheets and the other materials as she had promised. She reminded the students that although the week was structured in the plan, every plan could be improved. She invited them to comment on ways to make things better. "Remember," she encouraged them, "we are a learning team and equal partners in making learning happen. You know better than I do what would help you learn and understand better. You need to tell me your ideas as you think of them."

During the course of the week, as the students began this new routine, Lisa took the time to point out the different impression each activity was providing to reinforce their learning, both in class and as homework. By Wednesday, Jake had taken over that role, pointing out impression opportunities before Lisa could. It made her smile. They were tuning in to her concept and plan. The week ended with the first 100-point test. As students handed the tests in, they eagerly awaited their scores. Lisa had her key ready and corrected the tests as they were handed in. She allowed the student owners to immediately see their scores, but did not give the tests back. After all tests were handed in, the class spent ten minutes doing a project checkpoint check, a process they now had down pat after several weeks of practice. Lisa reserved the last five minutes of class for a quick feedback session on this first week of the load leveling plan. Some kids needed to see their test scores to finalize an opinion, but most felt it wasn't as scary as they had originally thought. The new question was how would next week's test with the review questions work. Lisa reminded them to hold on to this week's note sheets as a review tool.

As she headed home with her stacks of tests to finish correcting over the weekend, Lisa felt a sense of exhilaration. The process had worked, it seemed. She was leaving with all of her materials for next week ready and sitting on her desk, thanks to her extensive preparation during the summer. Lecture notes, artifacts, the dilemma question, Carmen Sandiego clues, visuals, and music from Mexico were ready to go. Outline maps, instructions, and note sheets were run off in quantity. And all that accomplished

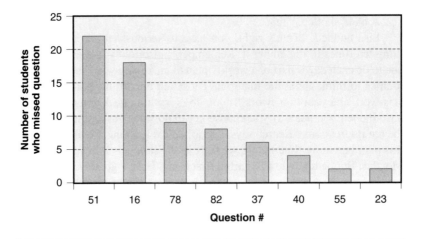

Figure 8   Pareto analysis of students' weekly tests.

in twenty minutes. The only prep left for the week was selecting newspaper articles and running them off. *Thank you, Bill!* she thought.

Lisa finished correcting her tests before she went to bed that evening and was generally pleased with the results. This was, she knew, a benchmark. She did the Pareto analysis and identified the top two areas with which the kids had problems (see Figure 8). She also noted what she wanted to change in her delivery to make that learning clearer. As she settled into bed for the night, she smiled in satisfaction. The plan had worked. *Now I have to make it work again.* And she did, week after week.

THE FIRST PROBLEM ARISES

"We have a problem." Lisa announced Monday morning several weeks later. "And you are going to be the ones who solve it."

Lisa outlined for the students in her classes how she had just found out that a Science field trip to the local environmental camp had been rescheduled and was now going to occur during their class time Thursday and Friday of that week. She had already been to see Todd to protest this invasion of her schedule and try to negotiate a different time, but had learned there was no other option. The environmental center had done the rescheduling, and these dates and times were all that were available for the trip.

"As you know, we have a schedule to keep. Losing two class periods in one week is tough. From the standpoint of completing our mission, I need to provide you with the information and give you an assessment of your learning—the test. Those two things have to be done. How we accomplish this is up to you. But whatever you decide, as long as it fulfills those two requirements, is going to be what we do. Majority rules, and we have to have the agreement of all the World Geography classes."

Students began to hash out possible alternatives and debate the pros and cons. Two best options were identified. The first was to postpone the test and take two tests the following week, one covering this week and the second covering the following week's material. While this option appealed to the procrastinators in the crowd, a good many students saw the danger in that solution.

"That's twice as much information that we have to study in one week," argued one student. "It will be harder to do a good job."

Lisa marveled at the broad thinking that was taking place. *Bill, I wish you could be here to listen to this,* she thought.

The second alternative was to go ahead and have lecture on Monday and Tuesday and take the test on Wednesday. This option also had skeptics.

"That means we have to do everything in three days, and we don't get a class to work on the map or review. That would be much harder."

In the long run, the procrastinators outvoted those who did not want to get behind. The same voting outcome occurred in all of the World Geo classes. It was agreed that two tests would be given the following week, one on Thursday and the second on Friday. The kids also decided to change the next Wednesday's schedule by using the entire class to review two weeks of material. Lisa made her plans accordingly.

The following week Lisa noted a lot of tension and unrest among the students beginning on Monday. A marked change in interactions and student appearance was obvious. As Wednesday approached she heard more students voice concerns, and even had several groups of students visit her privately. These students expressed high anxiety over the class decision for a double test week and how it would affect their grade. When Thursday rolled around, even the procrastinators who had voted for that solution expressed concern about how overpowering this week's task was.

Of course it's overwhelming, Lisa mused to herself, *if you waited until this week to start any of it.*

Friday's tests weren't any better than Thursday's had been. Almost everyone had done poorly on both tests. When she returned the two tests the following Monday, she called for team feedback on what had worked well and what needed to be changed. The discussion pretty much centered on the difficulty waiting had created in preparing for two tests in one week. Even those students who had voted for that option the week before acknowledged it had been a mistake. The consensus was reached by the students that they would never take that option again if a similar situation developed in the future. Immediately after the consensus vote was taken, Lisa noted a significant reduction in tension and a return to the good humor that had been the normal atmosphere in the class.

Later that evening, she reported the day's events to Bill. He listened to her story and marveled at the group dynamics she described, but it didn't fully surprise him.

"When people are empowered to make decisions affecting their own work, it is a natural tendency for some to take the route that appears easiest. However, it usually only takes one cycle of bad decision making that negatively impacts the decision maker for clairvoyance to emerge. Learning by mistakes is always the best teacher, Lisa. But you need to have the opportunity to make a mistake in order to learn from it. Your students have just learned a very valuable life lesson. Had you not empowered them to make the decision, they never would have learned what they did. So now, what's next?"

"I'm not sure, Bill. The plan seems to be working pretty well, and the kids appear to be relatively comfortable with it. We're getting the material covered, but there is room for improvement in performance."

"The ten impressions aren't getting the results you anticipated?"

Lisa's voice belied a challenge she had identified. "No, the kids who are actually using the ten impression research as a learning tool are doing fairly well. It's impossible to definitively say whether using it has improved their learning. I've never had them as students before, so I have no basis for performance comparison. I do know the class averages are up from the past two years. But I'd like to find a way to improve even what we are doing now. Do you have any suggestions?"

"Actually, I do. You and your students seem to have reached a level of comfort in working within your load leveling plan. Now it's time for your team to learn how to improve an improvement."

IMPROVING THE IMPROVEMENT

Bill briefed Lisa on two lean tools that he felt would accomplish precisely what she had said she wanted to do—improve the way her existing improvement plan was working. Lisa listened intently as her mentor explained how to use each of the tools, as well as how they could effectively be used together to effect continuous improvement. It was easy for Lisa to envision how to incorporate the tools into her existing plan, but Bill's clear and easy-to-understand description of how they worked sparked an idea she immediately presented to him.

"What are you doing tomorrow?" she blurted.

Lisa's question came out of the blue and caught Bill by surprise. "Um . . . working. Why?"

"I just got this great idea! How would you feel about coming over to school tomorrow and introducing these tools to the kids yourself and facilitating our team in trying them out?"

On the other end of the phone line, Bill felt his eyebrows rise and a slow grin creep across his face. He and Lisa had been talking about these kids for months. They had attacked an education problem together. But he'd been pretty much serving as an outside advisor and observer. This was a chance to work directly with the students and experience some of Lisa's challenge as well as her success. What an offer! It was one he didn't want to refuse.

"I'll tell you what. I'm locked into a meeting tomorrow. How about the day after?"

Two days later, on Wednesday, Lisa introduced Bill to her first World Geography class. She had forewarned the students the day before that Wednesday's regular class time use would be abbreviated for a special guest.

"Bill Baker is an improvement specialist," she began. "He helped me develop the learning plan and syllabus we are using so we could study the whole world rather than just part of it."

"Thanks, man," interjected Jake.

The students chuckled while Bill got an immediate sense of the potential enjoyment this opportunity was going to provide.

Lisa ignored Jake's remark and continued. "Mr. Baker has taken a personal interest in how our learning improvement plan has progressed and how we're operating as a learning team. He's been very impressed that seventh graders are collaborating to solve adult classroom management problems. And he thinks you're ready to tackle an even greater adult role in making our learning operation better. I think so, too. So he's going to show us some professional business methods to help us accomplish that. Let's give him a warm welcome."

The students responded with a round of applause as Lisa stepped to the side of the room and Bill moved front and center.

"Thank you very much, Ms. Randolph, for having me, and to all of you for that nice welcome," he began. "I jumped at the chance to come and work with you today. You know why? Because teenagers are natural-born innovators. You are full of great ideas, and you're not afraid to say what's on your mind." Bill shifted his gaze to Jake and nodded in acknowledgement of the young man's gumption. "Frankly, I love working with people like you because people with ideas are geniuses. Their ideas are what cause change, and only change can make things better. If nothing changes, nothing ever gets better." Bill let his compliment land completely with his young audience.

"Now, why am I here today? I spoke with Ms. Randolph a few nights ago, and she told me you all have adapted fairly quickly to the new weekly schedule and are handling it pretty well. She's interested in seeing what might be done to make it even better, but she's fresh out of ideas on how to accomplish that. I told her she didn't need to worry about where to find great new ideas—you kids have them stored right there in your brains. We just have to let them out. That's why I'm here. I'm going to show you how to tap into your own genius to make what you are doing in here as a learning team even more impressive, as well as make your job of learning even easier."

Bill leaned back on the worktable that had become so familiar earlier in the summer.

"I'm going to teach you to use two business improvement tools today. The first is called 'kaizen.' Anybody ever heard that word before?" A hand raised in the background. Bill called on the young Japanese student.

"I've heard my father use that word. I think it means something like improvement."

Bill turned to Lisa and commented, "You have one dynamite team in here, Ms. Randolph! Many adult workers I know have never even heard of kaizen."

Students in the class turned to give admiring glances toward Kozuko, who blushed with the unexpected attention.

"You are absolutely right, young lady," he responded. "Kaizen is a Japanese word that means 'little daily improvements.' In business, we get our work teams together for what we call a 'kaizen event.' We focus our thinking on solving a specific problem, and everybody brainstorms ideas on how to fix it. Sometimes the kaizen event can be done quickly, like in a class period. But kaizen on big or complex problems may require a week or more. We're going to do a down-and-dirty kaizen event today to find some ideas on how to make your job of learning easier and more effective.

"The second tool is called PDCA. It's easier for me to show you about this than just tell you about it." Bill stepped to Lisa's whiteboard and used some different colored markers to quickly draw four arcing and connecting arrows that formed a closed circle. He began labeling each arrow in its distinct color beginning at the top and moving clockwise as he described the markings he made (see Figure 9).

"You'll notice this diagram forms a circle. That signifies it's a closed cycle. It never ends. It just keeps going around in a continuous loop. It starts here at P. P stands for *plan.* The next step after plan is D for *do.* Then comes C for *check,* and the last step is A for *adjust.* Does this remind you of anything? Have you seen something like this before or heard these words before?"

Several hands were raised. Bill pointed to one of the responding students.

"Yeah, we use something like this when we we're doing experiments in Science."

Bill gave a thumbs-up for that answer. "Of course you do because this plan–do–check–adjust cycle is modeled after the scientific method, the same one you use to test hypotheses in science experiments. Using PDCA is just applying the scientific method to test a hypothesis about anything. It's a very simple way to test ideas and find out whether they're good or bad for solving the problem, whatever that problem might be. So today we're

Figure 9 Plan–do–check–adjust cycle.

going to use kaizen to identify ideas to make learning better in your World Geography class, and then we're going to use PDCA to determine whether the ideas work. Got it?"

The kids easily understood the simple concept. Over the next twenty minutes, Bill facilitated a brainstorming session with the students. He asked them thought-provoking questions. What makes it hard for you to concentrate in class? What would make learning easier? What would you do differently if you were Ms. Randolph? What do you need to do a better job of learning each week? Every idea was recorded on the whiteboard since, as Bill explained, every idea is a good one and must be respected, as well as the fact that one person's idea may spark an idea in someone else's mind. After the list was compiled, Bill reviewed each idea aloud. Students discussed, then selected the three top ideas based on their potential to improve learning or make their job of learning easier. Bill advised them to choose one of the three for testing, citing the restriction to one variable in a scientific method–based experiment. Lisa was stunned at the students' agreed-upon suggestion—give out the next week's materials on Friday. The rationale the kids offered was simple—we can get started on the material over the weekend if we want to.

The PDCA the students developed with Bill's guidance was simple and would be carried out over the next week or so. Plan = get the materials on

Friday to begin work on them over the weekend and ease the workload during the class week. Do = actually begin using the materials early as planned. Check = check to see if it actually eased the weekday workload *and* if test scores improved. Adjust = if it didn't work as you planned, is it worth continuing both from the individual and whole class standpoint?

Bill pointed out that their solution was a perfect example of the no- or low-cost improvements that kaizen is designed to bring forth. "Ms. Randolph will be running things off for you on Thursday night rather than Friday night or Monday morning. You won't be doing anything extra; you've just provided yourself with more time to do the same work. Congratulations! You've done a successful kaizen that captured an improvement idea and crafted a PDCA plan, all in less than an hour. I told you this was easy, and now you know how to use both tools to make improvements for yourself and for your class. Don't stop with just this one. These continuous improvement tools are meant to be used *continuously*! And I expect to hear about every single one of them!"

"I'll personally keep you posted if you give me your e-mail address, Mr. Baker," offered Jake.

"That's a deal, Jake. See me after class and I'll give it to you," Bill responded just as the bell rang. "Great job today, team!" Students filed out of the classroom engaged in excited conversation about what they had just done with Bill Baker, who was busy trading contact information with Jake. Lisa marveled at the simple but powerful process she had just witnessed, a process she would see repeated in the remaining World Geography classes that day.

Bill remained briefly after final dismissal.

"Well, what do you think?" he asked.

Slouched in her desk chair for the first opportunity to rest she'd had all day, Lisa shook her head in disbelief. "Never, ever would I have come up with the ideas they came up with. Giving out materials early. Running off an extra outline map for self-testing. And as you said, none of these ideas cost more time or money. I'm just amazed."

Bill smiled. "You really have no idea how powerful you have made your team today. You invited them to show you how to be a better teacher and how to improve classroom learning. You gave them a higher level of ownership and a more active role in the job of learning. I guarantee you that you will see more improvement in here than you anticipated, Lisa, in learning, in behavior, and in motivation. Schedule a classroom kaizen with some frequency. Build their skill in this area—knowing how to improve is a life skill. And it's applicable to anything."

Lisa's mind was moving, even if her body wasn't. "This whole experience and these two new tools have got me thinking in a new direction, Bill."

"What's that?"

"Well, the kids seem to have adapted well to the new class structure and routine, but for some kids learning is more difficult than it is for others. I've been thinking about how to help those more challenged individuals get better at learning in general, and I'm wondering whether it's possible to apply the lean waste elimination approach to the learning process itself. I have an idea I'm thinking about trying that I'd like to run by you."

Bill was interested in finding out more about Lisa's idea, and she explained it to the extent she had thought it out. Again, her logic and application of lean principles to the very basic learning process impressed him. "I think you should give your idea a try."

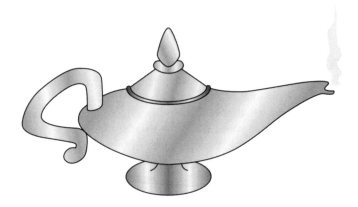

LEAN LEARNING

Drawing on her own knowledge of brain and learning theories as well as her classroom experience, Lisa knew that every individual has a learning style unique to his or her personality. The implication for teaching is sobering: no one human learns exactly like another.

A person's learning style is the set of preferences he or she is born with to most efficiently take in and process information—to learn. That's not to say that learning style can't be influenced in some ways over the course of a lifetime. Factors such as culture, age, and experience have been shown to impact the ease with which a person learns, but research has shown that the preferences a person is born with, especially in the area of information intake, remain his or her preferences for life.

Lisa's understanding was that learning style is a combination of brain dominance theory, intelligence theory, and common sense. *Brain dominance* essentially outlines the approach an individual takes to learning, while *intelligence,* or *talent,* identifies the tools a person has in their personal learning toolbox, and *common sense* directs how to effectively meld the two.

It seemed imperative to Lisa as a first step to improving individual learning that she would need to help the students discover their personal learning style. She had searched the Internet and discovered numerous self-assessment tests that were free, available online, and provide instant results. She tried several of them and decided on one to use with her students.

After the students had identified themselves as predominantly visual, auditory, or kinesthetic learners, Lisa explained that each style has its own toolbox of learning strategies. But because each student's style is unique to their individual personality, they would need a methodology to discover their personal best learning method. She developed the "Student Learning Kaizen Log" to help them go through the plan–do–check–adjust process. Dubbing her methodology Lean Learning, Lisa introduced it to her classes the next week. It was, she explained, kaizen, a process they already understood, only this time applied to learning.

From week to week the students formulated new ideas to improve their learning, based on their learning styles. They tested and refined those ideas using the PDCA tool they had learned from Bill, as well as strategies from their learning style toolbox, and they graphed their results. The students kept track of what they did to prepare for the quiz and developed a learning plan based on their learning style. Each student set their own quiz score goal. The measure of how well a student's plan worked was based on how closely the actual test score came to the targeted score goal. And then kaizen began again. Lisa emphasized to her empowered students that Lean Learning gave them control over their own learning.

Students who used the Lean Learning method with fidelity improved their learning performance significantly. Doing weekly kaizen on their learning process and sharing outcomes of attempted strategies with student peers both supported and motivated further learning improvement. Lisa witnessed a powerful transition as students advanced in self-discovery and took responsibility for their learning. The more successful they were in their learning efforts, the more eager they were to engage in learning activities. Success did indeed breed success.

THE PRINCIPAL'S DUE DILIGENCE

For Todd, as Metro Middle School's principal, parent–teacher conferences provided an infrequent opportunity to take what he considered a pretty revealing pulse of his school operation. As best he could, Todd cleared his schedule during the two-and-a-half days of conferences and spent a lot of his time in the hallways, talking to parents and students who were waiting for their conferences to begin or as they exited a concluded conference.

Todd found most parents, and students, for that matter, willing and eager to talk about the school experience as they saw it. There were, of course, irate people who would seek him out in his office with an issue they wanted resolved immediately. While he did hear and think about those messages, Todd felt the real story was one he would have to go after himself and solicit directly from the students and parents.

He had attended the open house parent night assembly during the second week of school and witnessed Lisa's introduction of her load leveling plan. He had heard the questions she fielded as well as the concerns that the parents had raised. In his opinion, Lisa had handled the session well. It seemed that most parents were open to giving the new plan a chance. Over his career, Todd had met few parents who didn't want a superior learning experience for their children. He also knew that most busy parents also appreciated not having to shoulder a lot of responsibility in their children's homework completion, especially middle school parents whose kids were very independent and didn't want parents checking on them all the time. Lisa's model had gelled with those parents when it was presented in theory, just as it had with the students when she first persuaded them to give it a try.

Todd had received frequent updates from Lisa on her progress throughout the summer and after school began. But he had also done due diligence by observing in her classroom several times. His visits were unannounced and made on a Monday, Wednesday, Thursday, and Friday so he could experience different facets of the class routine. What he found was the rigorous pace he had expected plus a consistently high level of student enthusiasm and engagement during each visit. But, Todd wondered, how did students and parents feel about this program now after several months of implementation, and especially after the first report card had been issued? So, during the first conference schedule of the year, Todd made a point of seeking out Lisa's World Geography families to solicit their feedback on the new class model.

"Hey, Randy, Charlie, Myra! How are conferences going?" Todd greeted three of Lisa's fifth-hour World Geography students who stood together just outside her classroom door engaged in quiet conversation.

The students looked up, smiled, and acknowledged their principal as he approached them.

"Hi, Mr. Winthrop."

Randy offered some clarification on his status. "Actually, I'm done with my conferences. I'm just hangin' out with these guys while my parents finish up with my sister's LA teacher."

"My conference with Ms. Randolph is in a few minutes," explained Myra. "Charlie's riding home with me. His Mom already had to get back to work."

"So you're all done?" Todd asked Charlie.

Charlie shrugged his shoulders. "Yeah. Ms. Randolph is the only conference we actually go to. I only came because I had to lead the conference."

Todd made a mental note and fished after some additional information. "You lead your conference?"

"In World Geo, yeah. It's no big deal, Mr. Winthrop. I went over my weekly tests with my Mom and showed her the test scores I graphed out so we could see my performance trend, then we talked about things I'm doing real well on and discussed some things I need to do better on. That's all."

"So it went pretty well?" asked Todd.

"Yeah, I think it went well. I think my Mom was actually glad to have me tell her everything and show her all that stuff myself. She said she was happy with how I'm doing."

Todd fished some more. "Well, are *you* happy with how you're doing?"

Charlie shifted his weight and lifted his head slightly as he contemplated the question. "Actually, I am, Mr. Winthrop. I was a little worried about this class at first, but I've got it covered."

"So the weekly tests are okay with you?"

Charlie nodded. "Actually, they're easier, I think. Don't you?" He posed the question to Myra and Randy, both of whom immediately agreed.

"We only have to learn about a note page of new information a week plus the major land features on the map we draw. And there are always some questions we've had before. But if I go over my notes each night, I pretty much know the stuff by the end of the week. I know I have to know it for Friday. I like having less to learn for each test—I can do better that way," commented Myra.

"If I have to take a test, I'd rather take one each week than try to remember three or four weeks worth of stuff," explained Randy. "I always figure I have time to study—the test isn't for three weeks—so I leave it till later and then there's too much to learn. My report card grade in here was better than I've ever done in Social Studies before. It's because I don't have the time to put off studying, and it doesn't take that much to do that ten impression thing."

"What ten impression thing?" asked Todd.

Myra piped in. "Ms. Randolph told us about how people have to have ten impressions of something before they can learn it for good. If we do the classroom activities and our homework, we get ten impressions in the week."

Suddenly, a voice came over the loudspeaker announcing the end of the current conference time. Randy's parents appeared from around the corner, and the door to Lisa's homeroom swung open as conferees departed.

"Gotta go! See you, Mr. Winthrop!" Myra greeted Lisa and, together, they walked into Lisa's classroom.

Charlie excused himself and headed down the hallway. And that left Randy and his parents in the company of Todd Winthrop.

"You ready to go, Randy?" his mother asked.

"Sure, but I need to get something out of my locker. Be right back." He disappeared down a side hallway.

Todd shook hands with Randy's mother and father. "Nice to see you again, Mr. and Mrs. Mancuso. Randy tells me your conference with Ms. Randolph was very positive."

Mrs. Mancuso smiled. "Yes, it certainly was. I liked having Randy being part of the conference so questions can be immediately addressed. I also think it's great to have the student do the report-out."

Todd continued his fishing, this time with the parents. "I know you attended the open house when Ms. Randolph first explained her new program. I'd love to get some parent feedback on how you feel it has worked for both Randy and you."

Both Mr. and Mrs. Mancuso contributed opinions that painted a positive experience in Todd's mind. They said they appreciated Ms. Randolph's specific recommendation early in the year to them as parents to have students focus on reviewing their daily notes for homework, as well as her explanation of how that strategy was critical to putting information into long-term memory. The limited and highly structured nature of the homework had resulted in a more positive experience for their son, who wasn't feeling swamped, as well as a very positive experience for them as parents. They weren't having to deal with nagging and the resulting stress that it had formerly brought on their family, plus Randy was doing well.

"To be honest with you," Mr. Mancuso confided, "the night she outlined the program at the open house, I wondered if it wasn't a little too much to expect from a seventh grader. I wondered how my son would respond to taking notes like he was in college, as well as weekly tests and a specific discipline of learning. But his attitude has been very positive about this class. He readily shares stories about what happens each day so we know what is going on in that class. We also feel very much a part of the learning process because part of our role is discussing an assigned issue with Randy each week for the Thursday class debate. He's coming home at night and reviewing his notes, working on his map, and he's realizing success. We're very pleased."

When Todd returned to his office at the end of the second conference day he had accumulated overwhelmingly positive comments from parents and students on Lisa's program model. In response to his most recent query, Lisa had assured him she was having no trouble keeping to the schedule she had originally set, and that the majority of students were performing well. If this continued for the rest of the year, Todd realized, it appeared that Lisa's plan to complete the delivery of her curriculum would be successful. But would the student learning performance scores go up? He was sure that the standardized test in geography in April would reveal the answer to that question. Before he left for the evening, he shared the parent and student feedback he'd gotten in a quick e-mail to Lisa.

REVELATION

As school years tend to do, Lisa's teaching year had flown by. Before she knew it, she was flipping her planner to the final week of her school plan. It was, she realized, already time to make preparations for the last week's activities. Unconsciously, Lisa's mind wandered back in time as she reflected on the highlights of the past nine months and her classroom experience with lean.

The previous summer's intense work on the planning and development of her curriculum seemed so far away and at the same time just like a month ago. She recalled the anxiety she had felt at first over how students and parents would respond to the rigorous new program. A smile crept across her face. She needn't have been so apprehensive. After figuring out how to put the plan together with Bill's guidance, implementation was all a matter of salesmanship and following the Golden Rule, with some diligence thrown in for good measure. She had sold the parents and students on giving the plan a chance with open communication and respect-based interactions . . . and unfailing enthusiasm, she admitted to herself. For the first time in her teaching career, Lisa felt she had really experienced the idyllic trust relationship and active collaboration with students and parents that is the goal of the "teaching triad."

What was left now was not teaching. That was done. She had completely delivered the entire curriculum. The load leveling plan had worked. And her students had done well. That didn't mean that everyone got A's. She hadn't expected that. She hadn't done the comparative analyses of class averages yet. She didn't need to go through that step to know that her students had learned more this year than last year or the year before. She had been able to finish teaching them about the entire world, not just a part of it. Even if they retained only 50 percent of what was taught that was 50 percent of 100 percent, not 50 percent of 70 percent, which is how much of the text she had covered last year. But Lisa was very sure her students would retain much more than 50 percent of their learning. She had faithfully followed the ten impressions strategy throughout the entire school year. The students in her classes who embraced that research-based methodology had achieved mastery learning. Those who hadn't routinely done the work hadn't fared as well, but she was convinced they had fared better than they would have if she hadn't embedded as many impressions in her standard teaching work as she had.

Standard work. She chuckled aloud thinking about how Bill had introduced those words into her life and how much a part of it they had become for her and her students. The pattern of the classroom work routine had become a very comfortable structure and discipline for everyone. Students knew without thinking what they would be doing on any day of the week, and they came prepared. They too had an expectation that the pattern would be maintained. It provided a familiar, secure system for the work of learning and teaching.

Empowerment. Omigosh, how the students had embraced empowerment! She recalled the first empowered decision-making session, the Science field trip fiasco of so long ago. The kids had eagerly taken on the decision-making role she offered and made a bad decision, a bad decision they never repeated during the other times a scheduling change decision was required. These 13-year-old students had become wiser through their problem-solving experiences. They had done improvement kaizen frequently and followed the improvement ideas with the PDCA methodology Bill had taught them. Improvement ideas were generated constantly now, and in fact, one of the materials she would prepare to give out this week was a kaizen outcome—a survey of her teaching effectiveness. Lisa had been intrigued when the class came up with the idea for a performance review of her teaching. The students, she knew, had no intention of using the survey to do anything but generate ideas on how she could help them learn better. The class had already done the survey once in the middle of the year. It was conceived as a way to improve the team's performance and had provided valuable clues for her own professional improvement.

Ah, yes, *team.* Without question her student groups had transformed into real learning teams. She recalled the resource sharing following each Friday's test. During those sessions, so much information and learning support was offered by her students to each other! She, herself, had learned about resources from them that she hadn't known existed! Somehow, in working together as peer collaborators, students and teacher had seamlessly blended into a truly successful learning "team" that could effectively tackle any challenge that came up.

Another realization for Lisa was that her seventh-grade students had become more active and self-directed in their learning. Note taking had made them better active listeners and improved their evaluative skills. They knew what they had to do to ensure learning—get ten impressions—they weren't just taking a stab at learning. They also had learned how to improve their own learning process. Students now had a method, a recipe for learning that, she believed, gave them a sense of security and capability. And that method was portable. The kids could take those understandings with them to subsequent grades and use that knowledge to be successful in other classes, too. The kids had the choice of whether to use those methods or not. Most had chosen to learn.

Her students had also experienced success. The apprehension they had expressed about being able to do everything in five days had long faded away. Week after week they handled the rigorous curriculum while maintaining a high level of enthusiasm. To say they looked forward to the Friday tests is an overstatement, but the students had long ago proven to themselves that weekly tests were no big deal and really were easier to handle than infrequent tests over more material. Lisa recalled with amusement how students impatiently waited after turning in their weekly test for her to correct them and tell them their score. They wanted immediate feedback to know whether or not their learning plan for the week had worked. Visual memories of their exhilarated faces lit up her own. Yet she could also envision the sobered faces of those whose plans hadn't worked out as well as they had hoped. But, she reminded herself, those students had hoped and cared enough to develop and try an improvement plan. Continuous improvement, she realized, had become her classroom culture.

What had started out as an experiment in applying lean to her classroom had gone way beyond Lisa's first intention. Bill had first come over to help develop a load leveling plan to enable her to completely deliver her assigned curriculum. The first day they had gotten sidetracked in a 5S workplace organization effort. Before she knew it, they added an empowerment element, which had led to her students doing kaizen improvements and tracking them with the plan–do–check–adjust cycle. That knowledge of the improvement process had expanded into applying lean to the student learning process as well as her teaching process. Everything had contributed to students becoming more successful learners. She felt she had become a much more effective teacher. So many positive outcomes had come from this one single initiative. Eliminating waste in everything had indeed been a worthwhile effort, she concluded. There was genuine cause for celebration.

As they filed into her classroom on Monday of the final week of school, Lisa sat on a tall stool at the front of the room and waited for her students to take their seats. Boisterous laughter and a tangible level of energy accompanied the animated youngsters as they entered these familiar surroundings and greeted each other and their waiting teacher. It was, after all, the last week of school. Students were giddy with the proximity of summer vacation mere days away. Lisa quietly took it all in. There was a bittersweet nature to the end of the school year. She was exhausted and looked forward to upcoming days of leisure and sleeping in. But, at the same time, she would miss the excitement and liveliness that being with these students brought to her life.

The bell rang and the students quieted down slowly. Lisa waited until she had their full attention.

"Obviously, we are done with World Geography lessons. I'm going to give you back last Friday's test. Unlike what we've done every other Monday this year, we won't spend class time going over the test questions, unless you want to. Do you?" she asked.

The students weren't interested. They knew their final test score had been recorded, that their grade for the term had already been determined, and more than likely their report cards were already prepared.

"As you know, today is the last day of regular classes. Tomorrow you will spend the entire day in your homeroom class except for after lunch when the whole seventh grade will meet down in the cafeteria for the Geography Bee competition. This class will compete in teams of eight against the other three seventh-grade World Geography classes. Tomorrow it will definitely sink in how much you have learned about this world you live in. I guarantee that you will amaze yourselves. The reason I am so sure is because of what I have seen you do and what we have been able to accomplish working together this year. I want to congratulate you, each and every one of you, for the hard work and effort you've put into studying World Geography this year. You have been truly amazing. You deserve this." Lisa stood and clapped for her class. Delighted with the praise, they joined their teacher and clapped for themselves.

"What I would like to do today is have a debriefing session with you about what we did in here this past year, to find out what you think was good, what needs to be changed, and get any ideas you might have to make things better. Are you up for a final round of problem solving?"

"Is this a reportable kaizen?" Jake quipped.

Everyone, including Lisa, laughed.

Lisa opened each class that day with a similar invitation to debrief. This was not a new activity for students accustomed to opportunity for improvement discussions on every facet of classroom operations. There was no need for Lisa to run the discussion. The kids were fully capable. From time to time she asked clarifying questions, as did students. Good-natured banter was interspersed with serious evaluations and idea sharing. Over the day of repeated versions of the first session, Lisa saw consensus on a great number of important findings, all consistent with her personal revelations. The way she had operated this year had proven as valuable to the students as it had proven valuable to the teacher.

The next day, after lunch, Lisa introduced the rules of the Geography Bee competition to all of the seventh-grade teams, each of which sat at a different cafeteria table. The competition had been a traditional last-day afternoon activity, for seventh grade as participants and eighth grade as observers, for many years. The principal and two seventh-grade teachers served as judges, another seventh-grade teacher kept score on a portable whiteboard, all of the eighth-grade teachers kept order, and Lisa was master of ceremonies.

The event normally featured 200 questions, more than Lisa felt could be answered in the two hours set aside for the occasion. It was run somewhat like a College Bowl, with teams collaborating to answer questions and a designated respondent to announce them. The team with the largest number of points at the end of the competition was entered in the state Geography Bee competition. That team also won a 24-pack of pop and a pizza party at the conclusion of the event.

Lisa had prepared questions in seven different categories that covered every aspect of geography study and quizzed understanding about areas and issues around the world. As the competition began, she noted the ease with which most teams were answering the questions, and with little need for lengthy discussion in selecting an answer. At the halfway point, she glanced at the scoreboard. She was surprised to see a close race and very high scores in relation to the number of questions she had asked. *I'm going to have to think up some tougher questions,* she thought to herself. At the conclusion of the competition, half the teams had missed less than twenty of the questions.

Before Todd officially announced the winning team, he congratulated the seventh-grade student competitors.

"In the six years I have been principal and judge for this competition, we have never had so many teams have such high scores. Congratulations to all of you. You really know your geography!"

Lisa was gratified by the competition's results, but Todd's aside to her at the conclusion of the competition warmed her heart.

"The achievement scores came in the mail this morning. Remember the geography score from last year and how you thought your plan would bring it up? It did, Lisa. Big time. I put a copy of the results in your mailbox. Congratulations!"

A FINAL MEETING, A NEW BEGINNING

As the teaching staff of Metro Middle School celebrated the end of a successful school year with coffee, juice, doughnuts, and bagels in the library the morning after students had been dismissed for the summer, spirits were soaring. Todd had just congratulated the faculty for facilitating improved school performance scores in reading, writing, and math.

"I really appreciate your concerted effort and focus on achieving the goals we set last spring. You did a tremendous job, so give yourselves a round of applause."

The teachers enthusiastically did.

Todd allowed them to bask in the warmth of their success before continuing.

"We also have another success to be celebrated. As you know, it was at this meeting a year ago that Lisa offered to pilot a new program in her World Geography class. She collaborated with a business improvement specialist to develop a teaching plan that would do two things. First, it would guarantee her ability to teach her entire textbook during the school year and complete the whole seventh-grade Social Studies curriculum. Second, the plan had to ensure that students would learn the material, not just be exposed to it. I'm not sure whether there is anyone here who is not aware of this, but Lisa succeeded in delivering her entire curriculum using this program plan not just in one of her World Geography classes, but in all of them."

Some of Lisa's colleagues stood up and clapped for her; those sitting in close proximity extended their hands in congratulation. And a few teachers expressed disbelief.

"You got through the whole book!?" they asked.

Lisa nodded in the affirmative while savoring the recognition of her professional friends.

Todd held his hand up to quiet the group down.

"What you may not have heard yet is how Lisa's model impacted her students' learning. In just one year our school's performance score in geography went from "Needs Improvement" to "Area of Strength.""

"What?!"

"For real?!"

"Holy cow!"

Todd went on. "This is no small achievement. I want to thank you, Lisa, for taking on what appears to be a very promising innovation to improve student learning. It certainly delivered remarkable results this year. Now the question is, can the achievement be replicated?"

Lisa responded enthusiastically. "I believe it can be replicated not only by me in World Geography, but also by other teachers in other classrooms. My plan is to use the model again next year. And I honestly think we should be looking at this on a whole school basis. If each one of us is able to deliver their complete curriculum, we all will benefit because then no one has to waste part of their instructional time teaching what wasn't completed the year or years before."

"Good," Todd replied. "I agree there is a longitudinal benefit to this that needs to be considered. Given the significant impact this pilot has had on student learning, I would like to expand testing it in additional classrooms beginning this fall. We need to determine whether or not it can deliver the same kind of results for other teachers and in other content areas. Lisa, I know you have documented everything you've done, would you be willing to assist other teachers in adapting the model to their classes?"

"Of course, and I know my mentor Bill would be happy to continue his involvement. I do want to say very quickly that this was not a difficult process. Most of the work is up front in the planning, and it actually made my job easier and less time-consuming once school started."

"Fine," Todd concluded. "I know this is the last day and you all are ready to get out of here, but I would like at least two volunteers who would consider teaming up with Lisa to develop a similar methodology for their classrooms beginning next term."

Tired teachers looked from one to the other. This was the time to be thinking about vacation, not the time to be thinking about new work. Some grumbling and mumbled comments were barely audible from an otherwise silent audience. Anne, an eighth-grade Social Studies teacher, spoke up.

"Lisa's students already understand the methodology and have had success with it. It seems logical for me to continue it forward. I'd be willing to explore this further."

"Thank you, Anne. Anyone else?"

Several moments passed. Todd knew that his teachers were reluctant to take on any more projects on top of the full plates they already had, especially at the end of the year, but he waited nevertheless, counting on another volunteer to step forward. To his surprise, Leo, the biggest and most vocal skeptic of Lisa's idea last spring, spoke up.

"We need to test this in another content area besides Social Studies. If I can do the up-front work during the summer while I'm not coaching, and it frees up my time during sports season, plus it improves student learning, I'll be willing to give it a try for next year in my English classes."

Normally not an eager volunteer, Leo's offer stunned everyone in the room. Todd expressed his sincere thanks to Anne and Leo, and asked them and Lisa to stay for a few moments after the staff meeting had been concluded.

"I really appreciate your dedication and leadership on this. Like I told Lisa last year, I will do everything I can to support your efforts. Let me know what you need, and I will do my best to assist you. I would like to participate in your planning process so I can learn more about it, especially if we are thinking about taking this schoolwide. So please keep me updated on when you are meeting so I can join you. Thanks again."

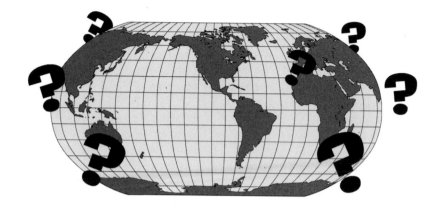

LISA'S EPILOGUE

Lisa's second year ran smoother than the first. Her new students and their parents had already heard about the empowered approach, success orientation, and the fun activities of the World Geography class. Because there was already a track record of success, her job selling the methodology was much easier.

As she had the previous year, Lisa succeeded in teaching the entire World Geography course, and continued to refine the syllabus. Metro's school performance score on the standardized geography achievement test again fell within the "Area of Strength" category, repeating the success of the prior year. Again in this second year of her load leveling and Lean Learning implementation, students took an empowered learning team approach. They eagerly embraced their role as full partners in classroom problem solving, kaizen, and continuous improvement activities. Lisa took great pride in her students' learning achievement, but she did not fully realize their level of learning mastery until the end of the second year of her new program.

Particularly gifted in quickly establishing trust relationships with students, Lisa frequently enjoyed visits from former students who would stop by her classroom just to say hello and update her on what was going on in their lives. So it came about during one such casual visit that her last year's seventh graders, now eighth-grade Civics students, seriously accepted her tongue-in-cheek challenge to a World Geography Alumni Meet against the current year's seventh-grade class. Jake, the quipster from the previous year, responded on behalf of his compadres with "Bring it on!" The match was set for the annual Geography Bee competition, which would be expanded to include eighth graders. Participation in the Alumni Meet was mandatory for current World Geography students, but would be optional for the eighth-grade Civics students. Her visitors assured Lisa that there would be multiple teams from their class who would take on her current students. They also took her up on her offer to provide four twenty-minute review sessions with the seventh-grade students.

Several weeks later, after the last of the 200 questions had been asked and answered at the World Geography Alumni Meet, Lisa and Todd were astonished at the results. With a full year away from the curriculum and less than an hour and a half of review, the best eighth-grade team narrowly lost the Alumni Meet by just 11 points.

BILL'S EPILOGUE

While Bill had successfully implemented lean principles, methods, and tools in other nonmanufacturing industries, he had never considered how they might benefit education until Lisa asked for his help. Through their collaboration he had gained an even greater appreciation for the versatility and applicability of lean.

Education is a system of processes revolving around the delivery of instructional services.

All processes can be improved. Lean with its waste elimination approach had proven every bit as effective at improving processes of education as it had in improving processes in other industries.

Lean tools might be adapted and applied slightly differently, but it was all a matter of selecting the right tool to match the challenge presented and desired improvement.

Bill's experience also underscored his belief in the positive outcomes of empowering people. He had seen firsthand how innovative Lisa's students had become once they were allowed to operate as process stakeholders in the classroom. They had gained ownership of their personal learning process and were empowered to improve it. Bill had seen the same outcome when adults in business were empowered.

While he had not used the term *hoshin planning* when helping Lisa develop her yearly plan to achieve her goals, Bill later explained that that's what she had done as a form of classroom strategic planning. As enterprises use hoshin planning to establish and align goals and ensure they are attained, Lisa had done the same. She had successfully done kaizen on her own teaching, and developed and implemented a level loading plan as an outcome. Takt time had proven relevant to teaching. They had used 5S to organize her workplace and standard work to make her and her students' work easier.

Bill had come in to teach kaizen and PDCA to Lisa and her students, and came away as the learner in how those tools can be applied to education. Lisa's development of her Lean Learning method was an application he was determined to implement in his own training classes.

Bill's involvement in the lean academic improvement that summer spurred Todd Winthrop's interest in broadened applications of lean at Metro Middle School. Bill's face became a familiar one in Todd's office as the two collaborated on improving operations while reducing costs through waste identification and elimination. It was for both men, and for the Metro Middle School community, the birth of an exciting new beginning.

Glossary

As Bill, Lisa, and Todd worked together to find lean solutions to education problems, they refined the definitions of lean terms to reflect education-related situations and the existing language of educators. The original definitions of lean terms as well as their education-specific definitions are contained in the following Glossary.

brain theory—Brain theory is the term collectively used to describe the findings of research on how brains work, and how they absorb and process information to understanding. These insights on what brains can or can not be asked to do to facilitate learning have provided educators with guidance on effective teaching methods, and students with similar guidance on effective learning methods.

checkpoint—A quality check done at a specifically designated milestone or point within a project or process. See *quality check*.

continuous improvement (CI)—Continuous improvement is a concise term describing the philosophy of organizational and/or personal development that advocates a never-ending quest to do better.

cumulative tests—Assessments that incorporate review questions on previously learned material to reteach and ensure that the ten impressions required for mastery learning are achieved. This strategy takes away what Lee Jenkins identifies as "permission to forget."

customer/end user—The end user of a product or service. Often, a process has multiple customers depending on the process step from which the view is taken. As an example, in the process of taking attendance, the first customer is the teacher who collects that information from the supplier (students or a parent phone call), but once that information is sent to the office, the teacher becomes the supplier and the office recipient becomes the customer. Each customer determines the quality of the product or service they received, whether it was complete or had errors, or was in an improper format and thus useless.

decision matrix—A chart that compares possible options and weighted selection criteria that is designed to help identify an optimal solution.

empowerment—The granting of authority and responsibility to do something. In lean, all school stakeholders, including administrators, teachers, personnel, students, parents, taxpayers, and community members, are authorized and empowered to engage in improving the processes of their work within the school organization. Empowerment must be real, be actively supported, and encouraged from the top down and the bottom up within the school organization if it is to be effective and sustained. Empowerment is also all or nothing—one can not be partially empowered or limited in their empowerment: either you are or you are not empowered.

5 Principles of Lean—The core principles of lean are:

1. *Value*: the worth something has in the eyes of the customer or end user as measured by his/her willingness to pay for it in time or money.

2. *Value stream*: the sequence of actions in which value is added to a product or service.

3. *Flow*: the logical sequence of activities in the value stream that leads from one to the next.

4. *Pull*: nothing is done until there is a need for it to be done.

5. *Perfection*: goal of getting better every day in the quest to ultimately be able to do something perfectly.

5S (workplace organization)—A methodology for organizing any workplace to facilitate the ability to do work efficiently by removing clutter, establishing a logical place for everything, and creating a system for maintaining the established order using five sequential steps that begin with the letter S. (A sixth S has recently been added: safety).

1. *Sort* refers to separating things into logical groupings.

2. *Set in order* refers to putting those sorted materials in a logical order of use.

3. *Shine* refers to cleaning and/or keeping materials in proper working order.

4. *Standardize* refers to keeping the established system the same unless change is warranted.

5. *Sustain* refers to doing what it takes to keep the established system going.

6. *Safety* refers to organizing the workplace in a way that does not jeopardize the safety of any workers or visitors.

flow—Flow is the logical sequence of activities in the value stream that leads from one to the next.

hoshin planning/policy deployment—A term for strategic planning at the organizational, department, grade, classroom, or even individual level that identifies a minimal number of reasonable goals to be achieved within a designated period of time, and the development of a tactical plan of initiatives and objectives by which those goals will be met.

ideal state—The state of things that, ideally, you would like to exist if everything went the way you wanted it to; the desired optimal end result.

impression—A feeding of information to the brain. An impression can be visual (seeing the information), auditory (hearing the information), or kinesthetic (physically manipulating something that will provide that information). Advertising research indicates that four separate impressions of information are necessary to get information into short-term memory, and a minimum of ten impressions are necessary to get information into long-term memory. Impressions are most powerful when they are distinct and separated in time, and when they occur in a variety of modalities.

interval—The time between the beginning of two separate measurements or occurrences. Lisa used her unit takt time (the time it took her to teach an increment of her curriculum) as her teaching interval because it matched the interval that offered her students the optimum chance to learn the material, their student learning interval.

kaizen—A term meaning "small, continuous improvement on everyone's part." The word itself comes from the Japanese words *kai* (small, little, good) and *zen* (good, change for the better). Kaizen is a focused effort by one or more parties to refine and improve a specific process or task. Kaizen involves brainstorming, analysis, and development of an action plan based on an improvement hypothesis that the plan will test and analyze. The process of kaizen can be used by individuals to improve a personal situation/process (for example, by Lisa's students utilizing Lean Learning) or by larger groups (for example, in the classroomwide kaizen led by Bill.)

lean—Lean is a term used to describe a value-added approach to process management of personal and work tasks. It considers the expenditure of time, effort, money, or other resources for any goal other than the creation of value as it is perceived by the customer/end user to be wasteful, and thus a target for elimination. See also *5 Principles of Lean*.

lean culture—An environment that is totally committed to continuous improvement, that empowers and encourages everyone to be problem solvers, that gives recognition for success, and does not lay blame for failure. A lean culture is based on respect for all people, for the work they do, and the essential contribution each person's work makes collectively to the overall work of the organization.

lean in education—A program of organizational improvement that empowers each and every worker in a school system—from student through superintendent—to increase his or her personal performance and job satisfaction through process improvement. Lean engages everyone in streamlining his/her work processes by identifying and eliminating the steps within each process that are wasteful, unnecessary, or do not contribute value to their work—or even prohibit it from being done. By incorporating a value-adding approach systemwide, schools can become more efficient in their operations and more effective at delivering their services, optimize the learning performance of all students, and create a culture of success and satisfaction for all.

Lean Learning—Lean Learning is a trademarked program by Lean Education Enterprises, Inc., that applies lean methodology to the learning process. It provides the methodology and means for students to take on an empowered and active role in the learning process. By applying lean to the learning process, students discover and do only what adds value to their learning process, and they become more efficient and successful at learning.

lean practitioner—A person who consciously or unconsciously implements lean tools and methods in the processes of their work.

lean teaching—By applying lean methodology to the processes of teaching, teachers can eliminate tasks that do not add value, and are thus wasteful, and focus their efforts on those that advance teaching and learning.

learning—The process by which people take information input into their brain and process it to new understanding by making connections of what they don't know to things that they know. The learning process can be optimized when the learner understands the best way to process information based on their individual personality and learning needs. Learning does not equate to teaching. Learning can fail to occur in the presence of teaching. The learning process, therefore, is related to but independent of the teaching process.

learning theory—Learning theory is the general consensus of how people learn based on the interpretation of research in that area. Learning theory consists of three elements: 1) brain theory, 2) learning style theory, and 3) the creation of a supportive trust relationship between the student and the teacher.

level loading/load leveling—In manufacturing, load leveling is sometimes referred to as *balanced production* since it is a method for creating an even flow in the creation of products and guaranteeing quality while meeting production deadlines. In education, level loading can be used as a planning tool to balance the delivery of instruction over a term to ensure that the assigned curriculum is completely covered. However, covering curriculum does not equate to student mastery of that curriculum. To be effective at ensuring that the delivered curriculum is mastered by students, it is essential to incorporate brain and learning theories into the development of the load leveling plan.

macro view—Measuring performance improvement at a higher-altitude view. Lisa used her school's standardized test score in her subject area to compare overall grade-level performance. The *micro view* is used to measure improvement at a lower-level view, more at the individual level.

mapping—A lean tool used to lay out process steps visually on paper so the process can be seen and wastes identified. There are a variety of types of mapping. *Process maps* simply lay out steps indicated with the use of labels and symbols. *Value stream maps* do the same but also identify where value is added. *Spaghetti maps* track the flow of movement as a process is carried out.

mastery learning—When students learn the curriculum in such a way that they understand and can recall it over time they are considered to have mastered that learning.

micro view—Measuring performance at a lower-altitude view. Lisa used her individual students' performance scores on the standardized school test plus their individual report card scores to determine whether each student had improved their learning performance. The *macro view* would be used to measure improvement using a higher-level view, at the classroom or school level.

mission/classroom mission—A logical goal for classroom work that defines the work itself, the rationale for why the teacher and student should engage in that work, as well as the personal return they each will gain from doing it. Classroom mission is often used synonymously with *classroom purpose.*

mistake-proofing—Sometimes referred to in Bill's world as *poka-yoke*, a Japanese word for "error-proofing." Any action or set of actions that are taken with the intent to prevent errors or mistakes from happening, along with the inherent need for resources to be wasted in fixing the error or mistake, is a form of mistake-proofing. In education, these can be check sheets, rubrics, parent sign-offs, or other means that help teachers, students, administrators, or parents ensure that all steps in a task or project are completed.

Pareto analysis—This is a statistical analysis tool that is based on the work of Vilfredo Pareto, an Italian sociologist and economist. The Pareto principle (aka the *80/20 rule*) states that 80 percent of problems are caused by 20 percent of the causes. Pareto analysis lays out the most frequently occurring problems to the least frequently occurring. This tool can be used to identify the most frequently missed test items (problems for student understanding) to indicate where remediation or improved efforts in teaching should be focused.

PDCA—plan, do, check, act (adjust) is the *Shewhart cycle* of process improvement, also known as the *Deming cycle.* This recurrent cycle of four steps is the foundation for any continuous improvement effort and is based on the scientific method for logically proving or disproving a theory. Simple to construct and use, the plan, do, check, adjust cycle makes evaluating an organizational or personal improvement an easy, straightforward, and perfectly provable task for adults, students, or teams.

perfection—Perfection refers to the continuous improvement goal of getting better every day in the quest to ultimately be able to do something perfectly.

process—A series of actions directed toward a specific goal. A process can also be a set procedure. Everything we do is a process or is made up of a series of processes. Being able to see a process and itemize individual process steps is necessary before the value of a process step can be determined and a potential improvement identified.

purpose/classroom purpose—A logical goal for work that defines the work itself, the rationale for why any individual should engage in that work, as well as the personal return they will gain from doing it. Classroom purpose is often expressed as a *classroom mission*.

quality check—A periodic evaluation of the fidelity of a process as well as the expected level of excellence or absence of defects in its product or outcome.

recycle questions—The repeated use of questions to assess particular learning to facilitate the required ten impressions needed to master it.

respect—A foundation and core tenet of lean is respect for all workers, the value of the work they do, and how it contributes to the overall goals and work of the organization at every level. Respect means that everyone is acknowledged for providing contributions of equal value to the organization, regardless of the work they perform. In a lean, respect-based approach to process improvement, all people are empowered and authorized to improve their work. And since no one is more knowledgeable about the work they perform than those who perform it, changes in the work must come from the process workers/owners, who understand intimately what impact or consequence the change will actually have on the process, and not be dictated by someone who is not personally engaged in that work itself.

rework—Work that must be done over because of a deficiency or error, thus a costly waste of resources.

rubric—An explicit set of criteria used to direct and assess the quality and completeness of a project to meet specific requirements.

standard work—An accepted set and sequence of activities needed to completely accomplish a task. This sequence becomes the "standard" best practice or way of getting the task done until an improvement can be made to the sequence. After any improvement is incorporated, the new sequence then becomes the standard practice, the standard way of operating, otherwise known as the *standard work*.

standardize—To make a framework consistent while allowing for a range of creative ways to work within the established framework.

strategic planning—Strategic planning is the process of identifying a minimum number of reasonable goals to achieve in a designated time frame(s) and the assignment of activities to support achieving those goals. *Hoshin planning* is a higher level of strategic planning that also incorporates the simultaneous development of tactical plans at the organizational level rather than passing on that responsibility as part of the goal assignment to department heads or managers as a subsequent activity.

streamlining—Streamlining work entails identifying and eliminating any steps within a process that are unnecessary or do not add value to the work, thereby saving the costs of waste and making the process more focused on reaching the stated goal.

systems thinking—A holistic view of process management that requires the ability to see the big picture of how processes are integrated and interdependent within an organization as opposed to viewing them as stand-alone entities. Systems thinking requires that a cause–effect perspective be taken in all decision making to ensure that organizational balance and health are maintained.

takt time—Takt time is the available time divided by the amount of work to be done. It is a set time during which a specific segment of material (course work) is delivered and assessed. A curriculum consisting of X units or chapters delivered over Y increments of time in a school year would establish the takt time. Takt time can be measured daily or weekly or monthly and is the metric for maintaining standard work. Lisa chose to divide her curriculum into segments that could be successfully delivered in one week—her takt time.

teaching—A process whereby opportunities to make the connections between what they know and what they do not know (learning) are created and presented to students; the management of those collective processes. The teaching process does not equate to the learning process.

Training Within Industry (TWI)—TWI is a program developed by the U.S. Department of War between 1940 and 1945 to quickly and efficiently help industries who were short on workers (due to conscription for the war) to train people effectively within a short span of time to be able to meet wartime materiel requirements. The training program was developed by training consultant experts on loan from the private sector. It focused on concisely providing exactly the instruction needed to complete the task, advocated that workers do problem solving to make the process better, and required from managers that workers be treated respectfully as individuals. TWI is the precursor of what is known today as *lean*.

value—Value is defined as the worth something has in the eyes of the customer or end user as measured by his/her willingness to pay for it in time or money.

value stream—The value stream is the sequence of actions in which value is added to a product or service.

value-added—In lean, anything that is essential to producing the desired outcome of the process is considered a value-adding element to it. If it is not essential to the outcome, it does not add value to the process.

visual control—The placement in plain view of all process elements and activities, as well as performance indicators, so that the location or status of each can be determined and understood at a glance by anyone.

waste—Waste is defined in lean as the unnecessary use of resources of time, effort, assets, talent, motion, processing, production, capacity, or knowledge that does not result in the addition of value to a process. Waste can also be anything that inhibits, delays, or interrupts completing the process successfully. Waste is not an easy thing to talk about in any industry, but especially in education. While people readily acknowledge that no one is perfect, it is very difficult for them to acknowledge that they could improve. That is often viewed as an admission of deficiency, or that their contributions are not valuable. The reality is, however, that no one is perfect and everyone *can* improve. Lean views waste on a strictly impersonal basis—the waste is found in the process, *not* the people. Lean also acknowledges that because this is not a perfect world, there will never be a time when waste doesn't exist. Not acknowledging that waste can and does exist in every process is unrealistic. That viewpoint will also prohibit the possibility for improvement.

wastes in education—Waste is anything that does not add value to accomplishing the goal. Waste is found in process steps, not in people. It can be anything that inhibits, delays, or interrupts completing the process successfully. There are nine categories of waste in education:

1. *Overproduction/effort:* The generation of more of something or of information than is needed at the moment, duplication not needed, redundancies, unwarranted changes for the sake of change that are not part of a continuous improvement activity. It can also

be just doing something before it is needed, consuming precious time that may be needed for another value-added activity.

2. *Talent:* The failure to recognize or develop, or to prohibit the use of, a person's talent, passion, or capabilities to the fullest; the underutilization or overutilization of a person's skills, abilities, training, and so on; not placing a person where they can and will use their knowledge, skill, and abilities to their fullest to benefit the organization or help others do the same through collaboration.

3. *Motion:* The unnecessary physical or electronic movement, searching, or transporting of items, people, or information that does not add value. If it is unnecessary, it is inefficient to do it.

4. *Time:* Idleness created when actions, information, people, or equipment are not ready when needed; unwise use of time, such as playing games versus doing work.

5. *Processing/handling:* Doing activities or tasks that are not really needed to accomplish the desired result, such as extra or unnecessary steps, or reviews, approvals, or requirements that are mandated but are not necessary.

6. *Assets:* Using more resources, money, inventory, books, people, facilities, or information than is needed. (That is, many people hoard items, order extra, spend money so they won't lose it from their budget, or don't utilize what they have.)

7. *Capacity:* The failure to realize full potential and experience its benefits. Capacity can be measured at both the individual and the organization level. The waste of capacity in education means not utilizing the full capabilities of the student, teachers, staff, and community to achieve the best possible educational opportunities and outcomes.

8. *Knowledge:* The re-creation of already existing knowledge. It can affect students and teachers and other staff. Knowledge waste can include poor planning, incomplete delivery or mastery of curriculum, redundant or omitted courses, poor organization or communication of information, or restricted possession of needed information by certain groups.

9. *Defects:* Human errors, honest mistakes, or any number of things that lead to work that contains inaccuracies or omissions or requires that it be done again (rework).

Additional Readings and Resources

Cleary, Barbara A., and Sally J. Duncan. *Thinking Tools for Kids: An Activity Book for Classroom Learning,* Revised Edition. Milwaukee: ASQ Quality Press, 2008.

————. *Tools and Techniques to Inspire Classroom Learning.* Milwaukee: ASQ Quality Press, 1997.

Connell, J. Diane. *Brain-Based Strategies to Reach Every Learner.* New York: Scholastic Inc., 2005.

Ewy, Robert. *Stakeholder-Driven Strategic Planning in Education: A Practical Guide for Developing and Deploying Successful Long-Range Plans.* Milwaukee: ASQ Quality Press, 2009.

Dennis, Pascal. *Getting the Right Things Done: A Leader's Guide to Planning and Execution.* Boston: Lean Enterprise Institute, 2006.

DuFour, Richard, and Robert Eaker. *Professional Learning Communities at Work: Best Practices for Enhancing Student Achievement.* Bloomington, IN: National Educational Service, 1998.

Eaker, Robert, Richard DuFour, and Rebecca DuFour. *Getting Started: Reculturing Schools to Become Professional Learning Communities.* Bloomington, IN: National Educational Service, 2002.

Fitzgerald, Ronald. *Smart Teaching: Using Brain Research and Data to Continuously Improve Learning.* Milwaukee: ASQ Quality Press, 2006.

Gardner, Howard. *Frames of Mind: The Theory of Multiple Intelligences.* New York: HarperCollins, 1983.

George, Michael. *Lean Six Sigma for Service.* New York: McGraw-Hill, 2003.

Harmin, Merrill. *Inspiring Active Learning: Strategies of Instruction.* White Plains, NY: Inspiring Strategy Institute, 1995.

Jenkins, Lee. *Improving Student Learning: Applying Deming's Quality Principles in Classrooms,* Second Edition. Milwaukee: ASQ Quality Press, 2003.

————. *Permission to Forget: And Nine Other Root Causes of America's Frustration with Education.* Milwaukee: ASQ Quality Press, 2005.

Jenkins, Lee, Lloyd O. Roettger, and Caroline Roettger. *Boot Camp for Leaders in K–12 Education: Continuous Improvement.* Milwaukee: ASQ Quality Press, 2007.

Lareau, William. *Office Kaizen: Transforming Office Operations into a Strategic Competitive Advantage.* Milwaukee: ASQ Quality Press, 2003.

Mann, David. *Creating a Lean Culture: Tools to Sustain Lean Conversions.* New York: Productivity Press, 2005.

Martichenko, Robert. *Everything I Know About Lean I Learned in First Grade.* Salt Lake City, UT: Signature Book Printing, 2008.

May, Mathew. "Lean Thinking for Knowledge Work." *Quality Progress* (June 2005).

Rother, Mike, and John Shook. *Learning to See: Value-Stream Mapping to Add Value and Eliminate MUDA,* Version 1.3. Boston: Lean Enterprise Institute, 2003.

Senge, Peter, et al. *Schools That Learn: A Fifth Discipline Fieldbook for Educators, Parents, and Everyone Who Cares About Education.* New York: Doubleday, 2000.

Sousa, David. *How the Brain Learns.* Thousand Oaks, CA: Corwin Press, 2001.

Spears, Steven, and Kent Bowen. "Decoding the DNA of the Toyota Production System." *Harvard Business Review* (September/October 1999).

Womack, James, and Dan Jones. *Lean Thinking: Banish Waste and Create Wealth in Your Corporation,* Second Edition. New York: Simon and Schuster, 2003.

Ziskovsky, Betty, and Joe Ziskovsky. "Doing More with Less: Going Lean in Education." Shoreview, MN: Lean Education Enterprises, Inc., 2007

About the Authors

BETTY ZISKOVSKY, MAT

Innovative and dynamic, Betty founded Lean Education Enterprises to bring the power of lean process improvement to schools. She is a licensed educator with over ten years experience teaching in urban and suburban environments. Betty introduced, adapted, and successfully implemented lean principles throughout her career, resulting in more effective learning by students. As a co-director of a Minnesota Charter school, she incorporated lean management in organization-wide operations, which led to increased collaboration, better communication among staff, and more efficient use of resources. Betty is a people person, an active listener, and energetically welcomes challenges. She is a national staff development presenter for the Institute of Educational Development and the Bureau of Education & Research, and a certified facilitator for the True Colors™ Basic Awareness Program. She has served as a member of the judging panel for the American Society for Quality's Education Team Excellence Award and currently serves on ASQ's STAR team to promote excellence in K–12 education teams. Betty is committed to providing all students with the world-class education necessary to compete in a global society. She is coauthor of "Doing More with Less: Going Lean in Education."

JOE ZISKOVSKY, MBA, CLM

Joe is the director of operational excellence for a multinational company and has served as an executive business administrator and manager for over 25 years. During that time he has been involved in applying continuous improvement principles to every facet of the business operation. He is certified as a Lean Practitioner, Lean Master, and Lean Trainer, and has served as an enterprise lean executive for ten years. Joe initiated, coordinates, and leads his companywide lean efforts at the domestic and international levels, and serves as a peer lean auditor for a large number of major Minnesota companies. Joe is a veteran kaizen planner and facilitator, and continues to develop innovative methods, training courses, and materials for applying lean to establish and sustain a lean culture and to meet organizational needs. Joe particularly enjoys his work as a senior consultant in applying lean techniques and culture in the K–12 education industry. He is the author of "A Guide to Managing Daily Improvement" and coauthor of "Doing More with Less: Going Lean in Education."

For more information about the concepts presented in this book please contact the authors at:

Lean Education Enterprises, Inc.
651-208-1293
bettyz@LeanEducation.com
or
joez@LeanEducation.com
Web site: www.LeanEducation.com

Index